Tomorrow's
Church

Tomorrow's Church

A Community of Change

John H. Westerhoff

Word Books, Publisher
Waco, Texas

TOMORROW'S CHURCH

ISBN: 0-87680-448-2
Library of Congress catalog card number: 76-2864
Printed in the United States of America.

Unless otherwise noted, all Scripture is taken from *The New English Bible*, © The Delegates of The Oxford University Press and The Syndics of The Cambridge University Press, 1961, 1970, reprinted by permission.

Quotations marked RSV are from The Revised Standard Version of the Bible, copyrighted 1946, 1952, and © 1971, 1973 by the Division of Christian Education of the National Council of the Churches of Christ in the U.S.A. and are used by permission.

For Judy and Pete

Contents

Preface

Tomorrow's Church is dedicated to Pete and Judy. Pete is Peter Gucker, an owner-director of the North Country Camps: Lincoln and Whippoorwill. Judy is his wife. They are my friends. It is August, and after having taught summer sessions at Toronto, Duke, and Fordham universities, my wife Barnie and I retreated to the Adirondack Mountains of New York and the solitude of Pete and Judy's winter cabin on the shores of Augur Lake to write this book. Each day I wrote; Barnie edited and typed until we were finished.

I share this because I want to explain why it was important for me to write this particular book in this place. Those of you who know my earlier works, *Values for Tomorrow's Children, A Colloquy on Christian Education,* and *Generation to Generation* are already aware of my debt to the progressive tradition. What you may not know is this: for me that tradition had its birth at Camp Lincoln many years ago. Pete's father, "Chief," now deceased, once taught at the Horace-Mann Lincoln School of Teacher's College, Columbia University. He founded these camps on the philosophy of John Dewey. From the age of eight, I spent two months each summer for twenty-eight years experiencing and living what I now identify as the best of the progressive tradition.

Of course, through the years, I have changed my perspective on and understanding of that tradition, but the genesis of my pilgrimage will always be fondly remembered. Now with my fortieth birthday behind me, I continue to struggle with the progressive tradition and its relationship to the Christian faith, the responsibility of the Christian in society, and the nature of Christian education.

This short tract is one more of my continuing attempts to reform our educational ministries in the church. I must admit that it was almost not written, for lately my mind has turned to other foundational issues in Christian education. But I was haunted by the awareness of a need for another call to a social understanding of Christian education, a call first given by my progressive mentor, George Albert Coe. And so with a three-week holiday in need of becoming for me holy days, I sat at my typewriter looking out over the trees and lake of my most memorable childhood experiences to pay a small debt to the past on behalf of the future.

Like my earlier books, this is not intended to be a definitive work. I am writing it for lay persons and ministers in local churches knowing that only you will write, with your lives, any truly important book on Christian education. My book of words therefore needs your reactions and actions. Only as those of us in the seminary, with the luxury of time to write words, struggle, dream, and create with you in the local church who have the opportunity to put words into deeds, will an educational ministry of the church, consistent with the gospel, emerge. May this book be a stimulant and an occasion for our working together. Be of good cheer! Have hope! I am convinced that if our memories of God's actions in history are renewed, if new visions of God's kingdom attract us, and if together we act responsibly with God each day, tomorrow can and *will* be different.

Keeseville, New York   JOHN H. WESTERHOFF

Introduction

Tomorrow's Church is not a typical book on church education. It is a special sort of book for a special group of Christians. And to be useful it needs to be used in special ways. I hope it is for you!

BY: Call me John. For ten years, as a United Church of Christ minister, I served parishes in Maine and Massachusetts. For the next eight years I served in the division of Christian education of the United Church Board for Homeland Ministries as editor of *Colloquy*. I am now associate professor of religion and education at the Duke University Divinity School.

FOR: Lay persons and clergy in local churches who are troubled over the relationship between the gospel and the world.

ASSUMES: Social action on behalf of justice, liberation, peace, and the unity and well-being of all persons is God's desire and intention.

RATIONALE: Churches need a resource to help them rethink and redesign their educational ministry for social change from a biblical perspective.

PURPOSE: To provide a resource for local churches on Christian education for social responsibility.

11

USES: A learning resource for use with youth and adults

A planning resource for leaders in the church's educational ministry

An action resource for programers of youth and adult Christian education

OUTLINE: Chapter one confronts the issue of the church and social action. Chapters two, three and four provide foundations for doing God's Word in society. Chapter five offers a model of church education for social change.

RESPONSE: This book was written to encourage feedback and discussion. Take notes. Raise questions. Note agreements and disagreements. Add opinions and ideas. Share your thoughts with others and with me. Reflect and act; act and reflect! Be faithful; *do* the Word!

Shalom,

JOHN H. WESTERHOFF

P.S. I hope you will write and share your thoughts and ideas with me, so I, in turn, can share them with others. In that way, this book can become a means of communication among and between many of us. My address is: Duke University Divinity School, Durham, North Carolina 27706.

Acknowledgments

No person is an island; I, least of all. Even many of my favorite ideas I owe to others, though I no longer remember who. Over the years many colleagues and friends inspired this book. As an act of gratitude and acknowledgment of my debt, I'd like to name them:

Frederick Herzog   McMurry Richey
Gordon Kaufman   Krister Stendahl
James Luther Adams   Walter Bruggeman
Bill Smith, my pastor   Herb Edwards

Edward A. Powers   Ted Ericson
Bob Burt   Charles McCollough
                Audrey Miller

of the United Church Board for Homeland Ministries.

And most of all, my wife, Barnie, who literally through her encouragement and labor made this book possible.

And our children:
Jill
Jack
Beth   for whom all my books are finally written.

Acknowledgments

Chapter One

Shipbuilding
The Challenge Before the Church

It was G. K. Chesterton who once raised the probing question, If you found yourself shipwrecked on an island, what one book would you hope to have brought with you? His reply is memorable: a book on shipbuilding. And that's the subject of this chapter. Why? Because I contend that the church is on an island, and Christians have forgotten their calling to be a seafaring people.

In the days of the apostles the church was characteristically symbolized as a ship with Christ as her pilot, tossed to and fro by the storms of history, riding the waves and maintaining her sure course. It's a beautiful image. But to continue the analogy, it seems that at some point we who claim the name of Christ took over the helm and ran the ship aground. That wouldn't be so bad, if subsequently we had not forgotten our seafaring days and come to believe that the island was our true home, and permitted the Bible, once our book on shipbuilding and navigation, to become a book on meaningful island life. From one point of view, that describes the problem facing the church and its educational ministry today.

15

Island Life

Will the world survive? Will our kind survive? I do not know for sure, but the more haunting question for me is, Who cares? or better, Who cares enough to do something about it?

We live in difficult days. I suppose that no one needs to be convinced of that. The mass media, our constant companions and informers, seem to strive daily to convince us of one all-encompassing doom after another, but in fact only numb us to an awareness of any crisis. Drugged by the reality of today it is difficult to get anyone to consider a long-range future. Most of us at best can only seem to live for today. Increasingly we adopt the hedonistic philosophy of eat, drink, and be merry for tomorrow we may die.

In the midst of the most serious recession since the Depression, Florida resorts were crowded with tourists. Business boomed. I asked why? The answer: many of those who had been laid off from work, whose labor contracts called for a number of weeks of continued pay, decided to enjoy themselves before it was too late. That was strange behavior for a nation reared on slogans such as, "Save for a rainy day." People are now living by a new slogan: "Buy now, pay later." Thus we live our crisis-filled lives locked into the present, strangely trusting that tomorrow will take care of itself. We no longer live for a visionary future and we have lost our memory of a meaningful past. Indeed, it appears that we lack a sense of hope because our best memories are only a collection of unrealized dreams and defeated desires. One more depressing problem engulfs us. We no longer possess a sense of power, a sense that we can make any real difference in this world, and so we have lost the will to act boldly on behalf of tomorrow.

Of course that is a caricature of our condition, but it does explain why so few of us are willing to struggle and sacrifice today in the hope that our actions might make a difference to the world a thousand years from now. By then our children and grandchildren will be gone. What does it matter what life is like for an unknown, unnamed child in Africa, Asia, India, or Latin America in 2976?

Why act today to affect life that will have no direct meaning for us or our offspring? But it is not that simple, is it? In the residues of our consciences we are haunted by Jesus' words, "If anyone wishes to be a follower of mine, he must leave self behind; he must take up his cross and come with me. Whoever cares for his own safety is lost; but if a man will let himself be lost for my sake, he will find his true self. What will a man gain by winning the whole world, at the cost of his true self?" (Matt. 16:24–26). So we make a few feeble efforts to show we care, but once again we are confronted by Jesus' words, "Why do you keep calling me 'Lord, Lord'— and never do what I tell you?" (Luke 6:46). And so the question surfaces: Is the church, the community of faith which claims Christ as Lord, helping us to build a ship and set sail with courage or is it only providing us with a drug to help us live painlessly on an island beset by human woes? I am not sure that I like the answer I hear. But I do know one thing. It was not always this way. The church once, inspired by God's Word, was a seafaring people.

I do not mean to sound morose about the present. By nature I am not a pessimist and I do not believe that everything is wrong with the church or the world. Indeed, I think we need to celebrate the good in the church and in modern life. But we cannot afford to ignore that which is not good either. It is complicated, of course. Some of the good things we have done have caused our problems. And some of our acknowledged evils have resulted from the good we have accomplished but still deny to a minority. Let us not overly condemn ourselves. Little will be accomplished by wallowing in tears of remorse or guilt. We are not an evil and corrupt people, though we are a sinful people. And our sin is, I suggest, a lost vision, a lost hope, a lost will to act. Those losses disturb me greatly. But I am joyful; as a person of faith, I am optimistic. I believe that God can remold the church's vision, reestablish its hope and restore its will to act. And I am enough of a possibilist to believe that you and I can help.

What kind of strategy will it take? I think it would help to try to understand the last quarter-century. Perhaps we are too close to it, but let me share a few generalizations. It seems as though the Christian church, for unknown reasons, became too popular in the 1950s. We lost our spiritual vitality and worldly relevance; we were lulled into a sleep of innocence. In the '60s, some of us began to dream dreams and our young saw visions. The church acted with courage in the world, but because we lacked a spiritual foundation we were easily disheartened by our lack of immediate success, discouraged by the complexity of issues, and disillusioned by the sinful nature of power (even our own). And then came the '70s with a retreat into the inner life, a search for moral and spiritual values in a community of care, prayer, and study. And a corresponding retreat from the world and social involvement.

Perhaps that is all understandable and necessary, but the challenge before us is to bring the 60s and 70s together and thereby repent of the 50s when we thought we were religious. The time is ripe and there is hope—for here and there, especially within the Black church, the Christian community of faith is coming to life, and where it is doing so, the gospel's vision, hope, and power are being revealed and witnessed to.

In these days it would be good for us to ask: What happened to the heritage left by our forefathers and foremothers? They came to this land inspired by faith with a vision of justice and freedom, of wholeness and community. I am aware that they tended to corrupt that vision by living for selfish ends, but is that any reason to cast aside the vision? They also came with the hope that they could build God's kingdom in their midst. True, they tended to neglect the reality of sin and forget that only God can bring in the kingdom, but is that any reason to give up all hope that life can be different? And yes, they came with a conviction that they could make a difference in this world, that they could contribute to a just future for all. To be sure, they tended to forget that unjudged power can corrupt and absolute power can corrupt absolutely, but is that any reason to lose all sense of responsible power and give up the will to act?

In the early days of this nation, our forefathers and fore-mothers went so far as to dream of a public school system that could help them realize their vision of a unified plural-ism where justice, liberty, and wholeness of life might be realized and each and every citizen use their power responsi-bly for the benefit of all. But something tragic occurred. While that vision was actualized for some, when it was no longer to the advantage of those who had realized its benefits, they developed excuses for not extending it to all, at least not immediately. When it was discovered that a great price would have to be paid, the rhetoric of their vision shifted to happiness in another world beyond the grave.

What about fore-fathers?

No longer troubled by an "eschatological itch," the church permitted the gospel to become a matter of personal piety and ignored its call to social liberation. Revivalism's backward look in support of the status quo took the place of evangelism's thrust into the future. A primary concern for nurture into ordinary life replaced the gospel's call of conversion to new life. Those who claimed Christ's name praised competition, at least those who could win did. They praised individualism, at least those who benefited from it did. And they praised aggression, at least those in power did, because that is how they had gained it and could main-tain it. And the church supported them in this distortion of God's vision, as well as in a corresponding distortion of the gospel's hope and power to transform the world. And many supported the church because it did not disturb their lives. Living on an island, they turned the Scriptures into a book about survival. They read their way of life into its message and, little by little, God's Word became their words.

Wrong you say! Hyberbole you exclaim! Perhaps, but do not miss what I am trying to say, namely, just because past visions were distorted, hopes dashed, and power corrupted, that is no reason to discard them. Instead let us bring the Scriptures back into the center of our lives. We need to be inspired and judged by God's Word so that we might once again be motivated by new visions, hopes, and the responsible use of power. But before that can occur, we need to consider what will be required in the way of a new crew, a new ship, and a new course for the church.

A New Crew

The early church remembered Jesus as the one who radically questioned people's lives and judged society's ways. His ministry broke open people's lives and set them on the path of a significantly different future. And those whose lives he transformed bound themselves into a community, the church, called to be the instrument of his mission in the world. With the advent of Jesus we witness the birth of a permanent revolution founded upon a profound dissatisfaction with the way things are in the individual and corporate lives of persons, and we discover a vision of what they might become. Jesus, therefore, taught his followers to question the existing religious and social order by bringing them under the judgment of God's intention.

Jesus calls us and the church to act for social change. But the church which bears his name sometimes forgets this. Jesus was a disturber. The question with which Jesus confronts Nicodemus is also the question with which he confronts us. That is, whether we are interested in the maintenance of religious and secular life as it is, or whether we are willing to embark with him on God's great redemptive enterprise in the coming new age.

Nicodemus, a teacher of religion, was well versed in the Scriptures, but blind to God's revelation. There is a Nicodemus in all of us. Indeed, there is more of Nicodemus in us than we want to admit. Our educational programs often suggest that to be Christian is to believe in God, to lead a reasonably moral life, and to be loyal to the church. We lose sight of the revolutionary character of the gospel. Recall that Jesus tells Nicodemus, a good religious man, that he must be born again. In an important sense each of us must be created twice—once when we are born and once when we repent and take on new courage to live in ways more acceptable to God.

The language of rebirth fills the New Testament. And Jesus answered, "In truth . . . I tell you, unless a man has been born over again he cannot see the kingdom of God" (John 3:3). And Paul wrote, "Leaving your former way of life, you must lay aside that old human nature which . . . is sinking towards death. You must be made new in mind and spirit, and put on the new nature of God's creating, which shows itself in the just and devout life called for by the truth" (Eph. 4:22–24).

We have often taken the call to repentance to others, but have neglected to hear its call to us. The church, like the world, needs to be converted. We need a new crew.

Where do we find this new crew? I contend that the church can no longer surrender to the illusion that child nurture, in and of itself, can or will rekindle the fire of Christian faith in persons or the church. We have expected too much of nurture. We can nurture persons into institutional religion, but not into mature Christian faith. The Christian faith by its very nature demands conversion.

In one sense we all inherit faith. Persons need to be nurtured into a community's faith and life. But persons also need, if they are to grow in faith, to be aided and encouraged to critically judge the faith they are given. Conversion then is best understood as a radical turning from faith given (through nurture) to faith owned. Conversion is radical because it implies ownership and the corresponding transformation of our lives. Only after a person honestly exclaims, "I believe," are they able to live the radical political, economic, social life of the Christian in the world.

Neither the pietist who has no commitment to the struggle for justice and righteousness in the world of institutional life, nor the social activist who has no personal commitment to Christ is converted to mature Christian faith. True conversion—authentic Christian life—is personal and social life lived on behalf of God's reign in the political, social, economic world. A person cannot be nurtured into such life. Not in this world.

Every culture strives to socialize persons to live in harmony with life as it is. The culture calls upon its religious institutions to bless such life and their educational institutions to nurture persons into it. But God calls us to be signs of *shalom*, the vanguard of God's kingdom, a community of cultural change. To reach the conclusion that such countercultural life is our Christian vocation and to be enabled to live such a corporate existence, in-but-not-of the world, necessitates conversion as well as nurture.

Church education for conversion means helping persons to see that they are called not only to believe the church's affirmation that Jesus is the Christ, but to commit their lives to him and live as his apostles and disciples in the world.

No longer may we preach peace of mind in this world or an individualistic salvation in another. The peace promised us in the gospel is a peace in the terms of this world, but a peace that is beyond human understanding. The gospel's peace results from a willingness to be crucified, personally and collectively, with Christ.

I gave a long lecture recently and an old man came up to me afterward and said, "Could you please tell me in one sentence what you mean by the Christian life?" I thought for a moment and responded, "To live individually and corporately under the judgment and inspiration of the gospel, to the end that God's Kingdom comes and God's will is done." I'll stick with that reply.

A theologian friend of mine once startled me by saying he found it very helpful to refer to Jesus as "oil head"—the anointed one, the Messiah. I asked why, and he explained that it reminds him that Christ is a title related to a function, a function once assumed by Israel's kings, then the prophets and last, but most important, by Jesus of Nazareth. And what was that function? To reveal to us who we are and what we are to become. I find that understanding full of insight. To affirm a living Christ is to look about us in history and see where that function is being assumed. For me that meant understanding the Pentagon Papers as a sign of Christ's living presence among us. Why? Because in those papers I came to realize what we as a nation were, and what we were called to become.

Individually and corporately we are called to live our lives under the judgment and inspiration of the gospel. It is a call, an invitation to discipleship, that can be accepted by both individuals and communities. In either case, it demands a yes or no response. There is no other choice. It is like someone asking you to marry them. To answer not yet, or sort of, is to answer no. We either accept or reject the invitation; there is no middle ground.

Regretfully many of us and many of our churches have tried to exist claiming the name of Christ without the necessary yes response to his invitation to take up our cross and follow him. But a partial response is a no response. Jesus does not ask us for our minds alone. To intellectually affirm that Jesus is the Christ is not enough. Neither does Jesus ask us for our emotions alone. To respond with our affections to his call for disciples is not enough. Nor does Jesus ask us for good actions alone. To behave in particular ways in response to Christ's lordship is not enough. Jesus asks for total commitment. He asks for our wills. He asks that we act with passion in thoughtful responsible ways toward all of God's creation. "Do you love me?" Jesus asks. "Feed my sheep." To love is to have passion. To feed Christ's sheep is to act. To love and to feed is to do God's will. And to do God's will is to have been converted to new life in Christ.

I contend that the reason so few adults in the church are involved in social action is that so few have a faith of their own. All of us must be nurtured in faith. Our faith first belongs to the community. We believe, but it is not yet our belief. Only after we have doubted and questioned the faith given us, can we be converted to a faith that is our own. Once we possess personal faith we are tormented and driven to put that faith into social action. The church today is composed of too many adults whose faith, while real, depends on the church and its authority. Christian education needs to help persons move from faith given through faith questioned to faith owned. That is what conversion is all about. And when the church is once again comprised of converted Christians, social action will be at the center of the church's life in the world.

The problem we face today, as in every day, is to make Christian education Christian. Some of us have forgotten the need of conversion along with nurture. Others have thought of conversion as only individual. Both have neglected the gospel.

Consider the Gospel according to John. The author of this Gospel understood the social nature of sin and salvation, the social message of the gospel. Christ came not only to convert and save persons; he came also to save the cosmos, the world. John's Gospel refers to Jesus as the Lamb of God who takes away the sin of the *world* (John 1:29). God so loved the *world* that he gave his only Son, that through him the *world* might be saved (John 3:16–17). Jesus is the Savior of the *world* (John 4:42). He is the light of the *world* (John 8:12).

The mission of the Christian is to transform both individuals and the social order. Christian education must be brought in line with the social message of the gospel.

"One Christian is no Christian," wrote Pascal. We cannot be Christian alone. We need a community of faith to nurture and support us. Each of us is both an individual and a member of some community.

A community is more than a collection of individuals. Anyone who has ever taught school or worked with a youth group knows that groups have personalities and wills just as individuals do.

We also know that groups have tremendous power over the individuals who belong to them. To remove an individual from a group and to change his or her life is one problem. But to return them to the group from which they came is to have them revert back to their old ways and understandings. Groups need to be converted as well as individuals. Society needs to be reformed as well as persons.

Indeed, we are more likely to change individuals if we can change the groups to which they belong than we are to change groups by concentrating on a few changed individuals. Surely if communities have personalities and wills, as individuals do, they can also be changed.

Both church and society need to be converted. To deny that truth is to ignore our social wisdom and the gospel. We not only need a new crew, we need a new ship.

A New Ship

How do we go about building this new ship? We have categorized too many persons and missed the truth in alternative understandings. We have insisted on either/ors rather than both/ands. In doing so the Christian church has been cruelly ruptured. We have pitted liberals and conservatives, evangelicals and radicals against each other. The church of Jesus Christ requires all four. Conservatives wisely remind us of the sacredness of the tradition, the wisdom of the past, and the centrality of the biblical story. Liberals remind us of the progressive nature of God's revelation, the importance of an open future and the need for change. Evangelicals have wisely guarded and proclaimed God's transcendence, human sinfulness, our need for redemption and the radically personal nature of faith. Radicals have wisely reminded us of God's immanence and the radical nature of Christ's call to responsible social action in the world.

The biblical faith does not know the exclusivistic categories by which the church has divided her people. Indeed, the gospel judges and calls us to unite in faith and strive together to live in the memory and hope of God's continuing action in the world. It demands that we join forces in a painful confrontation with both the world and the Scriptures. And it requires us to live harmoniously in the presence of the Lord of history.

Once again we have much to celebrate. Just as God is at work converting new disciples, here and there new communities of faith are emerging. One sign is a renewed understanding of evangelism. Recall the great nineteenth-century evangelists—William Garrison, Charles Finney, Theodore Weld, and Wendel Phillips. Each was a converted, committed Christian who knew that faith in Jesus Christ called for a social response. As evangelists, they led the antislavery movement and preached that the liberation of the soul was tied to the liberation of the slave, and only by a joint response could a person claim to be saved.

True, the revivalists who followed distorted the message of the evangelists. Looking only to the past and blessing the status quo they sought to save souls for eternal life, forgetting that salvation demanded significant changes in society as well as individuals, and that the kingdom was material as well as spiritual. To counter the revivalist's misunderstanding of the gospel, others in mainline Protestant churches took an equally erroneous position at the other end of the continuum.

Regretfully there are still some who as modern revivalists claim the name "evangelist." But the times are changing. The call of the new young evangelicals is a call to return to true evangelism. Those who wrote the Chicago Declaration, one of the great Christian documents of our times, and those who speak through the magazine *Sojourner* know that to proclaim and demonstrate the whole gospel of Jesus Christ with power is to enter and transform the political, social, and economic world. They know that to be faithful to the Scriptures is to become involved in corporate social action. Like the great evangelists of the past they preach a vision of God's kingdom and a call for discipleship which transforms both individual and corporate life. Correspondingly, many of us within main-line Protestantism have discovered our spiritual poverty, and rediscovered the authority of the gospel message and its call to conversion.

United in a grappling with Scripture we have come to realize that preaching peace in our nation is not enough. We have learned that the gospel is addressed to institutions and nations as well as individuals. National self-interest is an enemy of peace. So is nation worship, international economic domination, racism, classism, sexism, ethnocentrism, and the reliance on military solutions to world problems.

Peace is a gift of God, a gift that comes when we humans act to meet the conditions of peace which God has established. God therefore calls us to national penitence and new life. No longer can we permit the values of competition, individualism, and aggression to dominate our national life. No longer can national self-interest rule our decision-making. Instead we need to turn our national priorities over to global needs and become the advocates of liberation for all who are oppressed and, by identifying the marginal peoples of the world, strive for social justice.

Of course, salvation cannot be earned; the crucial test of its genuine presence is, as always, ethical and social. "The man who says, 'I know him,' while he disobeys his commands, is a liar and a stranger to the truth; but in the man who is obedient to his word, the divine love has indeed come to its perfection" (1 John 2:4–5). "My children, love must not be a matter of words or talk; it must be genuine, and show itself in action" (1 John 3:18).

Revelation combines both words and deeds. God speaks and acts. The biblical narrative is both show and tell. In words the Scriptures witness to the action of God. Together they form the Word.

Words mean little apart from action. A character in *My Fair Lady* sings "Don't talk of love, show me." Words are necessary but they are not enough. On the streets it is sometimes expressed crudely, but accurately: "Put your money where your mouth is."

God did not only come in Jesus of Nazareth to tell us about salvation. God died on a cross to show us the limitlessness of grace. God continues to witness through word-in-deed in prophets and apostles. The church is called to be a witness for God in a similar way—through words-in-deeds.

Remember, the heart of the gospel is not speaking; it is an action. Paul makes that very clear when he points to the crucifixion as the heart of the gospel message. It is the action, not the words, of Christ which is a stumbling block (1 Cor. 1:23–24).

We who follow Christ are required to take up our cross and do as Christ has done (Mark 8:34). The church is not required to talk. Rather it is to act with Christ. We have distorted the gospel by letting it become a matter of words. In the church, we have been content to communicate with words alone forgetting that God's Word is an identifiable action.

Words are at best symbols for experience and our experiences are always a result of someone's action. At their worst, words are signs or definitions. To differentiate, let me give an example. You are told that a red light means stop. It is a sign and you have been taught its definition. But does it affect your life? Let us say that most often you stop when you see a red light, but on occasion you neglect its message. One day while proceeding through a red light you are struck by an oncoming car, and you are seriously injured. I'm sure that in the future, whenever you see a red light your foot will go quickly to the brake. Because of your experience the red light has become a symbol. It now has power over your behavior. The only way the Word of God can become a symbol for the world is through the church acting according to its truth.

For example, you can tell someone you love him/her and that love means caring and respect for his/her personhood. But if prior experience has taught this person that the word "love" means being used, your message will not be understood and your verbal definition will have little significance or meaning. Only if, over a period of time, you repeat the word "love" and act toward him or her in a caring respectful way will they come to understand the meaning that word has for you. We all know that, but we do not always act accordingly.

The words of Scripture become the Word for others when they are acted upon by us. As the body of Christ, the church is called to act with Christ in the world so that the world might experience the gospel.

To accomplish that mission the church is required to live in-but-not-of-the-world. Of course that is not easy to do. We need a new ship. Every society asks of its religious institutions that they bless the way things are. That is why those churches which support the status quo are often most popular. Though they deny the gospel, they fulfill the world's demand that they be communities of cultural continuity.

Christ calls his church, however, to be a community of change, to act with God in transforming the world into the kingdom of our Lord and Savior Jesus Christ. To make an adequate response to that vocation is to live simultaneously in this world and in the kingdom. We cannot escape from the world and be faithful. Neither can we become so enmeshed in the world that we lose our souls. To live on the boundary is difficult and demanding. But the biblical story provides us with a guide.

The Scriptures remind us that we are a special people with a peculiar memory—a memory of being continuously called to leave where we are and go somewhere else and be someone else, a people never staying put or holding on to present understandings and ways.

We are a people with a peculiar vision—a vision of a world not yet realized and yet already come. In our worst moments we stop envisioning and believe it is well to celebrate and keep life as it is, but God haunts us by promising us a new age and pulling us toward its realization. Continuously God demands that we be dissatisfied with life as it is. God judges us and provides us with a vision to inspire and stimulate us to action.

And we are a people with a peculiar hope—a hope that gives meaning to life as a pilgrim seafaring people on a mission under the power and purpose of the gospel. It is a hope which proclaims that persons and institutions can change, that people and the public order can be transformed to more fully embody God's will for justice, harmony, liberation, community, and peace.

If as a reformed community of faith the church is to live in these peculiar visions and hopes, if we are to act in the world as the body of Christ, we will not only need a new crew and a new ship, we will need a new course.

A New Course

A number of years ago I attended a meeting on social justice, liberation, and peace. Bishop Theophilus of the Mar Thomas Church in India was with us. He spoke of the efforts of his church to minister to the material and spiritual needs of persons caught in the throes of hunger and poverty. He spoke of the need for a more global understanding of the gospel so that our comfortable churches in the West might recognize their common mission with Christians who labor in the midst of oppression and injustice. Then someone raised a question. What specifically could we do in our churches in the United States? "Read the Bible" was his reply. Well, perhaps that answer should have been obvious, but it was not. And there lies the crux of our problem.

Of course, Bishop Theophilus was not advocating a simplistic sort of Bible reading in isolation from the cries of suffering and injustice. Nor was he suggesting that Bible reading was an end in itself. Rather he was urging us to begin our consideration of the church's mission with a renewed understanding of our identity as the pilgrim seafaring people of God. He was urging us to consider the church as a community of faith living under the judgment and inspiration of the gospel, the good news of what God has done, is doing, and will do to bring in the kingdom of justice, unity, community, liberation, welfare, and peace.

Bishop Theophilus is not alone in this emphasis. Strong new voices of liberation and social justice from Asia, Africa, and Latin America are rich in biblical imagery and insight. These churches have seen the biblical vision through new eyes. They have regained the gospel's hope that God is the advocate of the poor, the oppressed, the hurt of this world. And they have accepted the power-filled gift of the Holy Spirit to reshape the church's actions to meet the needs of a broken world.

In the United States our problem is twofold. Some of us have, for all intents and purposes, ignored the Scriptures; others of us have distorted its message to support our own sinful understandings and ways. All of us need to be cured of our blindness so that we might once again return to God's Word and hear its message of hope for the world, that is, its message of judgment and mercy.

To look at the Bible through new eyes and to hear its redeeming message through new ears is to comprehend afresh that the message of salvation is related to both the material and spiritual needs of persons and society.

The prophetic message of God to the church today is as of old: "Hear . . . you that are deaf; and you blind men, look and see" (Isa. 42:18). It is a message to conservatives and liberals, evangelicals and radicals. We have all sinned, each in our own way, but if we turn again to the Lord he will abundantly pardon and say: "Blessed are your eyes, for they see, and your ears, for they hear. Truly, I say to you, many prophets and righteous men longed to see what you see, and did not see it, and to hear what you hear, and did not hear it" (Matt 13:16–17, RSV).

God, we are taught in the Bible, is the God who acts in history. We being created in the image of God are called to be historical actors as well. Our uniqueness as human beings lies in our power to make history, to will God's will and in some measure determine with God the future. For that end God created us. We, therefore, fulfill our humanity insofar as we join God in kingdom-building.

God will build the kingdom. We are to live for the kingdom. By acting together, God's kingdom comes. Of course we do not know exactly when or how it comes. Nor can we be sure of its specific character but we can strive for its realization and thus be faithful to our calling.

The kingdom of God is the righteous rule of God in a redeemed society where the vision of *shalom* is fully realized. *Shalom* is the Hebrew word frequently found throughout the Old Testament. No single English word can convey its full meaning. It includes not only responsible relationships among people but also responsible use of the natural world— the vision of God's ultimate intention for all creation revealed through people, a vision of unity, well-being, community, justice, liberation, and peace.

This kingdom of God is not "within" us (Luke 17:21, KJV), a private religious experience of peace of mind. It is rather "among" us (NEB) and in the "midst" of us (RSV), an individual and social phenomenon. Here and there it is present among us, and for it we hope. Daily then we pray "Thy kingdom come, thy will be done on earth as in heaven" (Matt. 6:10).

We are called to be a community of visionaries with Christ who live individual and corporate lives motivated by the vision of the kingdom, and in the hope that we act with God for its realization. Social change is the dynamic process through which we are pulled forward by our vision of God's kingdom and pushed from behind by our memories of God's continuing activity in history. Thus we stand each day on the threshold between the past and the future.

Christian life in this world is lived to the end that God's will be done and God's kingdom come (Matt. 6:10). We ought not refuse to accept the responsibility given us by longing for another world or being satisfied with the world as it is.

Being Christian is not living some special style of life called religious, but it is living as an agent with God in the transformation of the world into what God intends for it to become. We do that by witnessing through word-in-deed to God's vision, by living with hope, hope which comes from an awareness of God's action among us, and by assuming responsibility for the power God has given us to join in history-making.

As Christians we know that both individual and social life has meaning and purpose. God acts in history through people. History, therefore, is directional and intentional. We are called to fullness of life as citizens in God's kingdom who having accepted social responsibility with God are willing to assume the cost of discipleship. Our salvation cannot be separated from discipleship. We cannot call Jesus "Lord," if we do not do the things Christ commands (Luke 6:46). To be a new creation in Christ Jesus is to share God's vision and purpose for life, to have accepted the cost and joy of discipleship, and to live each day in the hope and intention of acting to fulfill God's will.

God's will is for both individuals and society. That is why the Christian faith has never ignored the principalities and powers, though the church has sometimes done so. Pietism, that is, restricting religion to the immediate relations between an individual and God or to an individual's relationship with another individual, is heresy. To neglect the world and institutional life is to deny the sovereignty of God over the whole of life, and is a form of idolatry. To confine God to our personal existence and the Christian life to personal behavior is in effect to leave the world to the principalities and powers. And that is a denial of the lordship of Christ.

According to the biblical narrative, the power of God was working in its most characteristic and decisive way when the children of Israel were being liberated from bondage in Egypt. That was the first exodus. The appearance of Jesus Christ and the emergence of the early church was the second. Recall also that the prophets railed against both the sins of individuals and institutions. From a biblical perspective our covenant with the Lord of history entails responsibility for the total character of society. The cult of privatization represents a pious form of turning away from the Lord of history—and that is sin. Surely there is no gospel that is not a social as well as an individual message of good news. The responsibility of the Christian convert is as always, therefore, a responsibility for society.

In our most recent memories there have been two quite different responses to God's call to Christian responsibility. The first was the liberal progressivism of the social gospel with its commitment to the gradual human transformation of society through human action. Following a disillusionment over the assumption of inevitable progress and human goodness came neoorthodoxy with its focus on human sin and a shift from political and social change to an emphasis on the redemptive acts of God in history, on judgment and realism. Each possessed partial truth. Each was a corrective for the other. Neither alone was adequate. Both have been caricatured and criticized by advocates of the other and by those who shared neither of their understandings of the social dimensions of the gospel.

What is needed today is a new understanding that has no blind expectations of progress or belief in the capacity of human beings to build God's kingdom. Founded upon a more radical understanding of God's action in history and a renewed social consciousness consistent with the biblical narrative, we need to work toward the equipping of persons and groups to engage in responsible action in society. That, I suggest, is the new course the church needs to take and its educational ministry support.

The next three chapters will reflect my understanding of the vision, hope, and power which need to undergird a viable educational ministry for social change. The last chapter will present a model for church education for social responsibility. Together these chapters present my understanding of church education for the converted Christian who within a community of faith is striving to do the Word by engaging in responsible Christian social action.

Chapter Two

Visions
The Future from God's Perspective

Our society, the church included, is largely without visions, which means without clear and adequate goals. The result is rootlessness and instability. And that is what our life on our little island has become. God did not create us to be island dwellers. God created us to be the vanguard of the kingdom. We need to rebuild our ship and set sail with Christ. However, we will never be inspired or enabled to do that without a vision. Therefore, one of the central tasks of church education today is to help us regain a vision of God's kingdom.

That vision is not unreal. It is a motivating force, a hope by which to live, and a direction in which to travel. Throughout Scripture the people of God, when they are most faithful, live by God's vision for them and the world. But "where there is no vision, the people perish" (Prov. 29:18, KJV).

Life is made meaningful and purposeful, hope is born and nourished, and our actions judged valuable—good or evil—because we have goals toward which we live and are willing to die. That is why the Word which Jesus brings to us is so important. We need to be reminded that until we have once again owned God's vision, we will remain lost and doomed.

Jesus' Word centers on a realizable vision. "After John had been arrested, Jesus came into Galilee proclaiming the Gospel of God: 'The time has come; the kingdom of God is upon you; repent, and believe the Gospel' " (Mark 1:14–15).

Those words summarize the content of Jesus' preaching. All of Jesus' words and actions are to be understood in the light of this proclamation of the imminent kingdom of God. The miracles are signs of the kingdom; the parables and other teachings describe life in the kingdom and the conditions of membership.

There is a striking difference today between the preaching of the church and the preaching of Jesus. Generally we have lost the centrality of the kingdom of God. That loss is recent. The kingdom of God was a central motif in American history from the Puritan divines to the social gospel. Some say that our past understandings were simplistic, dangerously naïve, and even heretical. Perhaps so, but to ignore the centrality of the kingdom because of past misuses is surely unreasonable, if not unfaithful.

In terms of the gospel, the vision of the kingdom of God is both a gift already given and a goal for which to live and hope. In God's good time it will fully come; we are called to live today in and for its promise. It is a vision worthy of our lives and deaths; to that truth Jesus testifies. God's vision is not a dream of pie-in-the-sky-bye-and-bye, or a drug making it possible to accept the way things are. It is a present worldly reality. And because it has already come, it provides us with meaning for yesterday, purpose for today, and hope for tomorrow.

Surely, God's being cannot be separated from God's will or activity in the world. God is the power of the future, a future known in today. Today *is* yesterday's tomorrow. In one sense the future is always hidden; in another sense it is revealed in the events of yesterday and today. The kingdom has come, is coming, and will come. The kingdom of God, therefore, provides us with a vision which is concrete and real.

Church education must once again be focused upon the development of visionaries who have committed their lives to Jesus' vision of God's kingdom as *the* future for the world and all humanity.

The church is not simply a group of individuals with common interests and conviction. The church is a community in communion with a living Christ dedicated to the kingdom of God. It is a community proclaiming the imminence of that vision, living in the hope of its anticipated coming and giving its life as a sign of its reality. To witness in word and deed to the gift and promise of the kingdom is the church's vocation. The church's sin is its distrust and disbelief in God's future. Until we have changed our ways of thinking and committed ourselves to living and dying for the kingdom of God, the church will not know salvation.

Accomplishing that goal will not be easy. Most of us have difficulty envisioning any future. We find it especially difficult to envision the future with God. Some have lost their ability to envision. Most of us live in the present. We are encouraged to do this. We even define the future in terms of the present. The farthest future we imagine is tomorrow and it is not expected to be especially distinct or different from today.

We have been taught to distrust or ignore our dreams. And we have been discouraged from dreaming. "Face reality" we are told. Education has not encouraged or even enabled us to fantasize or imagine. Our intuitive modes of consciousness have been left to atrophy.

When we are taught to conceive the future, it is in terms of reasoning what tomorrow is *apt to be* through a logical projection of the present or by reasoning what tomorrow *can be,* based upon a scientific analysis of the present.

Most often we fall into the future or get carried there by responding to some current crisis, a recommended "new" panacea, or our faltering attempts at problem-solving. Is it any wonder that the future is not significantly different from the present, except perhaps more so? Only if we can once again have our imaginations enlivened; only if we can once again begin to envision a new desired future, beyond anything we have known, will the future be different in terms of peace, justice, community, well-being, unity, and liberation. Indeed, the Scriptures themselves will remain outside our comprehension for they are an expression of the intuitive and a witness to the centrality of a poetic vision for the life of faith.

As church educators our challenge is threefold. First we need to provide a learning environment which nurtures our God-given ability to dream, imagine, fantasize, create, and envision. Second, we need to find the means to sustain and transmit the biblical vision of God's *shalom* kingdom within a learning and witnessing community of faith. And last, we need to devise ways to help persons and the church to use God's vision as they prepare for and engage in Christian social action.

The kingdom of God—God's vision for this world and all peoples—must become *our* vision! To that need we turn.

Advent

Advent is a season of waiting and preparation. But waiting and preparation for what? For the birth of Jesus? Yes and no—only insofar as that birth signals the coming rule of God which is the end of all alienation and oppression. Advent appropriately celebrates the announcement of the new rule of God with its revolutionary implications for persons and society. Not a popular message perhaps, but honest to the Scriptures.

The message of the prophet Isaiah is delivered to a community—a people rather than an individual or even a collection of individuals. It is a message to a people who have, amidst bondage and oppression, been waiting for a redemptive act of God. Listen carefully to Isaiah:

Comfort, comfort my people;
—it is the voice of your God;
speak tenderly to Jerusalem
and tell her this,
that she has fulfilled her term of bondage . . .
(Isa. 40:1–2)

And what shall occur? The poetry is beautiful and speaks for itself, but we should not miss its political, economic, and social overtones:

Every valley shall be lifted up,
every mountain and hill brought down;
rugged places shall be made smooth
and mountain-ranges become a plain.
Thus shall the glory of the Lord be revealed,
and all mankind together shall see it . . .
(Isa. 40:4–5)

The message of Isaiah is good news to an oppressed people: God is coming to rule and along with this reign is a reward for those who have been injured and hurt:

He will tend his flock like a shepherd
and gather them together with his arm;
he will carry the lambs in his bosom
and lead the ewes to water.
(Isa. 40:11)

Few of us are bothered by Isaiah's message until we realize that it may not be for us. Or perhaps a better way to put it is this: The truth in Isaiah's message is for all people, but that message is to be understood differently by the "haves" and the "have nots," that is, unless we are to fall into the sin of preaching what Bonhoeffer called "cheap grace" or what Marx and others rightly recognized as the "opiate of the people."

The Bible is a double-edged sword. It brings a message of mercy to the "have nots" of this world and a message of judgment to the "haves." Think about it.

The Gospel according to Luke quotes from our Isaiah text. John (the Baptist) is in the wilderness and God speaks, telling him that God's people need to prepare for the coming of the Christ who will usher in God's kingdom. As preparation they are to repent and their repentance is to take the shape of new actions in the world. So when the crowds come to John to be baptized, he delivers these harsh words to them:

"You vipers' brood! Who warned you to escape from the coming retribution? Then prove your repentance by the fruit it bears. . . . Already the axe is laid to the roots of the trees; and every tree that fails to produce good fruit is cut down and thrown on the fire" (Luke 3:7–9) .

"Comfort, comfort my people" is a message to the oppressed, suppressed, depressed, and repressed peoples of this world. It is a message proclaiming the downfall of the "haves" —those who presently have advantage, power, well-being, and possessions. There is no comfort announced for the comfortable. The coming of God in all glory is for the "haves" a message of judgment. The Word of God announces a revolution, a turning upside down, a leveling. At long last those who hunger and thirst for justice and righteousness, those who have been without the blessings of God, are going to be satisfied; they are going to receive from God that which all God's people, as a birthright, deserve—namely, justice, liberation, well-being, community, and peace. God's act of judgment puts things right. It establishes justice and mercy for those who do not have it.

We may not like that message, but unless we intend to sugar-coat or dilute the Word of God we had better hear it. When God puts things right, the last are going to come first and the first last. Jesus, remember, spent little time trying to convert religious people. Instead he went straight to the social outcasts and thereby changed the constituency of the kingdom.

If such radical language bothers you, read Isaiah again:

> The Lord will go forth as a warrior,
> he will rouse the frenzy of battle like a hero;
> he will shout, he will raise the battle-cry
>   and triumph over his foes.
>   Long have I lain still,
> I kept silence and held myself in check;
> now I will cry like a woman in labour,
>   whimpering, panting and gasping.
> I will lay waste mountains and hills
>   and shrivel all their green herbs;
> I will turn rivers into desert wastes
>   and dry up all the pools.
> Then will I lead blind men on their way
>   and guide them by paths they do not know;
> I will turn darkness into light before them
>   and straighten their twisting roads.
> All this I will do and leave nothing undone.
>   (Isa. 42:13–16)

There lie God's words of judgment on the "haves" of this world. God's words of mercy for the "have nots" is of another sort.

> How lovely on the mountains are the feet of the herald
> who comes to proclaim prosperity and bring good news,
>   the news of deliverance.
>
>   (Isa. 52:7)

Recall the moving words uttered by Zechariah at his son John's birth:

> Praise to the God of Israel!
> For he has turned to his people, saved them and set them free,

and has raised up a deliverer of victorious power
    from the house of his servant David.
So he promised: age after age he proclaimed
    by the lips of his holy prophets,
that he would deliver us from our enemies,
    out of the hands of all who hate us.

(Luke 1:68–71)

And of his son John, he exclaims:

And you, my child, you shall be called Prophet of the
  Highest,
for you will be the Lord's forerunner, to prepare his
  way
    and lead his people to salvation through knowl-
      edge of him,
    by the forgiveness of their sins:
for in the tender compassion of our God
    the morning sun from heaven will rise upon us,
to shine on those who live in darkness, under the
  cloud of death,
    and to guide our feet into the way of peace.

(Luke 1:76–79)

Once again we hear the announcement that a time is coming when those who have been without peace will know peace, when the hurt, the "have nots" of the earth, will be granted justice and mercy. At that time God will put things right and the hope expressed in the early prayer of the Didache will be answered: "O Lord, let this dirty earth go to pieces and let Thy kingdom come." Judgment in the Scriptures is a day looked forward to, a day when God establishes justice, that is, when justice is given those who have lived with injustice. For the rest of the world the day of justice is a day of judgment, a day of gloom and doom.

Nevertheless the Word of God remains one word. It is the message of God's will for *shalom* and the establishment of God's rule on earth. Recall the song that Mary sings after Elizabeth recognizes that Mary carries in her womb the fulfillment of the Lord's promise to the world. And Mary sings:

> Tell out, my soul, the greatness of the Lord,
> rejoice, rejoice, my spirit, in God my saviour . . . .
> his mercy [is] sure from generation to generation
>   toward those who fear him;
> the deeds his own right arm has done
>   disclose his might:
> the arrogant of heart and mind he has put to rout,
> he has brought down monarchs from their thrones,
>   but the humble have been lifted high.
> The hungry he has satisfied with good things,
>   the rich sent empty away.
>
> (Luke 1:46–47, 50–53)

From Christmas to Epiphany

Like the end of the calendar year this season marks an end and a beginning. In one sense it announces a definite end of the old and a radical new beginning.

> . . . no child shall ever again die an infant,
>   no old man fail to live out his life;
>   every boy shall live his hundred years before he
>   dies . . . .
>   Men shall build houses and live to inhabit them,
> plant vineyards and eat their fruit . . . .
> They shall not toil in vain or raise children for
>   misfortune. . . .
> The wolf and the lamb shall feed together
> and the lion shall eat straw like cattle.
>
> (Isa. 65:20–25)

The new can be expressed only in the poetry of the peace-able kingdom. The mistake we so often make is in trying to turn the Bible into a literalistic document. The Bible is not science minus, but poetry plus. Little understanding will be gained from asking *what* specifically do its words mean? Like art, music, dance, and poetry the wiser question is *how* does it mean?

Here in the moving words of Isaiah we have a dramatic picture of *shalom,* of the kingdom of God, an earthly manifestation of heaven established among us. We do not know concretely and specifically what that kingdom will look like, but we do know its character and shape. And in the event of Christmas, in the mystery of a baby born in a manger, we sense through the eyes of faith that it has come among us.

And for whom has it truly been an Epiphany? Perhaps not those who come first to our minds, those within the community who historically bear the privilege of transmitting the faith's story. Recall the account in chapter 13 of the Book of Acts. A large crowd of people who were not part of the community of faith had gathered to hear Paul and Barnabas. But the members of the community became jealous and angry. They did not want to believe that the message of the kingdom was for anyone but themselves and those who become one of them.

We should be somewhat sympathetic. Christmas has boldly announced that for God's people salvation has come, the kingdom of *shalom* has arrived. But who are God's people? Is it not a fact that in the Scriptures "God's people" always refers to the oppressed, repressed, suppressed? Are not the chosen people of God those who have not known justice, who have been oppressed and injured by the system? Are not the true children of God the Afro-Americans, the Mexican-Americans, the first Americans and others in our midst who have been prevented from receiving the blessings of God the rest of us take for granted?

It would be well for us who are desirous of believing the vision which God brings to all humanity to realize that it is especially meant to be a joyful vision for the little, weak, hurt people of the world. That may make us angry, but it ought to call our lives into question. And our faith.

One other word needs to be spoken concerning the vision by which Christians are called to live. That word is found in the Gospel according to John (John 16:16–24). Jesus is explaining to his disciples that in a little while they will see him no more, and then again in a little while they will. The disciples we are told wonder what he means and Jesus explains: "You will weep and mourn, but the world will be glad. But though you will be plunged in grief, your grief will be turned to joy. A woman in labour is in pain because her time has come; but when the child is born she forgets the anguish in her joy that a person has been born into the world. So it is with you: for the moment you are sad at heart; but I shall see you again, and then you will be joyful, and no one shall rob you of your joy" (John 16:20–22).

For many today, Jesus' explanation still leaves us with questions. Recall then that Jesus' coming establishes God's kingdom. In Jesus *shalom* is given, but it is not yet achieved. We need to be reminded of that. The "have nots" of this world have reason to weep and the "haves" have reason to be glad, but a day is coming, says Jesus, when the tide will finally turn and the promise of the kingdom given to the "have nots" will be realized and their joy will be full. And we should add, the final judgment on the "haves" who have not repented and become the advocates (those who give their lives in the struggle for *Shalom*) of the "have nots" is also coming and they will experience the pain of God's final judgment.

From Epiphany to Lent

The vision of the *shalom* kingdom by which the church is called to live her life is founded upon rigorous demands of obedience. It is appropriate during this interim period of the church year to articulate the price to be paid by those who would live in and for God's vision.

The opening lines of the vision received by Isaiah confront those of us who have benefited from God's promises with our corporate sin, our rebellion against God's will for God's world. Throughout the Old Testament we are reminded that God's gifts carry responsibility. "Take care not to forget the Lord your God and do not fail to keep his commandments, laws, and statutes which I give you this day. When you have plenty to eat and live in fine houses of your own building, when your herds and flocks increase, and your silver and gold and all your possessions increase too, do not become proud and forget the Lord your God who brought you out of Egypt, out of the land of slavery" (Deut. 8:11–14).

And what is the proper response to our memory of God's past deeds of justice and mercy? "You must fear the Lord your God, serve him, hold fast to him" (Deut. 10:20). "You must carefully observe everything I command you this day" (Deut. 8:1). And what does God demand, "Only to act justly, to love loyalty, and to walk wisely before your God" (Micah 6:8)—that is, to act with God, as God acts, toward all God's people.

And the vision of what God wills for all humanity is clear: "For the Lord your God is bringing you to a rich land, a land of streams, of springs and underground waters gushing out in hill and valley, a land of wheat and barley, of vines, fig-trees, and pomegranates, a land of olives, oil, and honey. It is a land where you will never live in poverty nor want for anything" (Deut. 8:7–9).

It remains for those of us who know of God's promises to imitate God. We serve the Lord of the kingdom by providing blessings to those denied them. Recall Jesus' remarks about the sheep and the goats (Matt. 25:31–46). Who is it that truly love the son of God? Those who feed, clothe, shelter, and care for the needy of this world. "I tell you this: anything you did for one of my brothers here, however humble, you did for me" (Matt. 25:40).

Of course there is a price to be paid by those who would be children of God's vision. ". . . no person is worthy of me who does not take up his cross and walk in my footsteps. By gaining his life a person will lose it; by losing his life for my sake, he will gain it" (Matt. 10:38–39) says Jesus.

How much has the church of Jesus Christ avoided announcing in word and deed this vision of God's kingdom. Simply reflect on your individual and corporate life within the world as one who claims the name of Christ; then reflect on Jesus' words:

> How blest are you who are in need; the kingdom of God is yours.
> How blest are you who now go hungry; your hunger shall be satisfied.
> How blest are you who weep now; you shall laugh.
> How blest you are when men hate you, when they outlaw you and insult you, and ban your very name as infamous, because of the Son of Man. On that day be glad and dance for joy; for assuredly you have a rich reward in heaven; in just the same way did their fathers treat the prophets.
> But alas for you who are rich; you have had your time of happiness.
> Alas for you who are well-fed now; you shall go hungry.
> Alas for you who laugh now; you shall mourn and weep.
> Alas for you when all speak well of you; just so did their fathers treat the false prophets (Luke 6:20–26).

Once again we must ask to whom the vision is directed and what is our proper response? The Word of God continues to be misunderstood and the vision corrupted by our misunderstandings. Remember that while Jesus spoke to himself these words, "Man does not live by bread alone," to the hungry he responded by giving them bread. We eat too much and quote Scripture to the hungry. At least through our actions, we do. And that brings us to Lent.

From Lent to Easter

It might be well to begin this season of the church year with a word from Jeremiah and Paul. Jeremiah had a vision of God at war with us. "For the Lord has spurned the generation which has roused his wrath, and has abandoned them. . . . From the cities of Judah and the streets of Jerusalem I will banish all sounds of joy and gladness . . . for the land shall become a desert" (Jer. 7:29–34). And Paul presents a vision of God expressing love for us. "Then what can separate us from the love of Christ? Can affliction or hardship? Can persecution, hunger, nakedness, peril, or the sword? 'We are being done to death for thy sake all day long,' as the Scripture says; 'we have been treated like sheep for slaughter'—and yet, in spite of all, overwhelming victory is ours through him who loved us" (Rom. 8:35–37).

The proper response to Jeremiah's vision is repentance; to Paul's, faithful acts of justice for the oppressed. The Christian is daily confronted by the need for both. The role of the biblical vision then is much like that assumed by a good newspaper editor: To comfort the afflicted and afflict the comfortable.

In any case, our sin is our refusal to believe or accept the cost of God's vision. God's Word is clear—we are to turn about, reform our ways with all our neighbors, restore our vision of the unity, peace, and the well-being of all people, and then respond to God's call for justice and liberation.

With Amos God cries:

> Let justice roll on like a river
> and righteousness like an ever-flowing stream.
> (Amos 5:24)

And with the psalmist, God exclaims:

Turn from evil and do good,
    seek peace and pursue it.
        The eyes of the Lord are upon the righteous,
        and his ears are open to their cries.
    The Lord sets his face against evildoers
    to blot out their memory from the earth.
When men cry for help, the Lord hears them
and sets them free from all their troubles.
The Lord is close to those whose courage is broken
and he saves those whose spirit is crushed.
The good man's misfortunes may be many,
the Lord delivers him out of them all.
    He guards every bone of his body,
and not one of them is broken.
Their own misdeeds are death to the wicked,
    and those who hate the righteous are brought to ruin.

The Lord ransoms the lives of his servants,
and none who seek refuge in him are brought to ruin.
                        (Ps. 34:14–22)

We have used those words of the psalmist to dull our consciences. Too often we have substituted spoken prayers of justice and liberation for acts. We had better think again. Hear Isaiah:

        When you lift your hands outspread in prayer,
    I will hide my eyes from you.
    Though you offer countless prayers,
        I will not listen.
    There is blood on your hands;
        wash yourselves and be clean.
    Put away the evil of your deeds,
        away out of my sight.
Cease to do evil and learn to do right,
pursue justice and champion the oppressed.
                      (Isa. 1:15–17)

Can we make the case stronger! The vision of God is clear; the oppressed, repressed, depressed, suppressed people of the world will, in God's time, be granted wholeness of life. Those who do not advocate their cause and act on their behalf will know the wrath of God, for God's kingdom of unity, peace, well-being, liberation, and justice for all people comes on earth.

What must God do so we will hear that Word? In Jesus of Nazareth God came to us and announced the good news. Recall Jesus in the synagogue. He stood to read the lesson and read from Isaiah:

> The spirit of the Lord is upon me because he has
>   anointed me;
> he has sent me to announce good news to the poor,
> to proclaim release for prisoners and recovery of
>   sight for the blind;
> to let the broken victims go free,
> to proclaim the year of the Lord's favour.
>
> (Luke 4:18–19)

And then what did Jesus say?

> Today in your very hearing this text has come true.
>
> (Luke 4:21)

But do we believe that? Jesus went through the streets teaching the good news of God's kingdom come.

> How blest are those who know their need of God;
>   the kingdom of Heaven is theirs.
> How blest are the sorrowful;
>   they shall find consolation.
> How blest are those of a gentle spirit;
>   they shall have the earth for their possession.
> How blest are those who hunger and thirst to see
>   right prevail;

they shall be satisfied.
How blest are those who show mercy;
    mercy shall be shown to them.
How blest are those whose hearts are pure;
    they shall see God.
How blest are the peacemakers;
    God shall call them his sons.
How blest are those who have suffered persecution
    for the cause of right;
    the kingdom of Heaven is theirs.

                               (Matt. 5:3–10)

He also pointed to the signs of the kingdom's coming. When John the Baptist sends friends to ask Jesus if he is the one who is to come, Jesus answers: "Go and tell John what you have seen and heard: how the blind recover their sight, the lame walk, the lepers are made clean, the deaf hear, the dead are raised to life, the poor are hearing the good news . . ." (Luke 7:22–23).

The writer of Matthew's Gospel tells of Jesus going from town to town announcing the good news of the kingdom and curing every kind of ailment and disease. The sight of the people moved him to pity: they were sheep without a shepherd, harassed and helpless. And he sent out the disciples with these instructions, "Proclaim the message: 'The Kingdom of Heaven is upon you.' Heal the sick, raise the dead, cleanse the lepers, cast out devils" (Matt. 9:35–10:8).

The disciples were to live in and for God's kingdom. The same charge is given to us. And just as the Bible is biased toward those who are denied the kingdom's blessings—the poor, the oppressed, the hurt, the captive—so are we to have the same bias. When God's blessings are denied anyone, God's will is thwarted. Wherever structures or acts of injustice deny opportunity and well-being to individuals or groups, God's vision is denied.

Throughout the Scriptures the vision of that which is and is to be, is central to the life of the faithful. Wherever racism, sexism, classism, or militarism exists, God's kingdom is thwarted.

Wherever there is community, unity, wholeness, peace, economic justice, racial justice, political justice, and the liberation of the oppressed, there the kingdom of God is signaled.

Easter announces that the principalities and powers which have prevented the kingdom's coming are defeated. In this season it would do well for us to repent for not living as if that were true. It would do well for us to celebrate our faith by renewing in our hearts the vision of God's kingdom and by committing our lives to live in and for its completion. Then and only then will both the "haves" and the "have nots" together know the blessing of God, the parent of our Lord Jesus Christ and our parent.

From Easter to Pentecost

In this season of Easter it would be well to recall and to celebrate the prophecy of Zechariah:

> Rejoice, rejoice, daughter of Zion,
> shout aloud, daughter of Jerusalem;
> for see, your king is coming to you,
> his cause won, his victory gained,
> humble and mounted on an ass,
> on a foal, the young of a she-ass.
> He shall banish chariots from Ephraim
>   and war-horses from Jerusalem;
> the warrior's bow shall be banished.
> He shall speak peaceably to every nation,
> and his rule shall extend from sea to sea,
> from the River to the ends of the earth.
>   (Zech. 9:9–10)

With Jesus Christ came abundant life for all people (John 10:10). Jesus is the world's true liberator. He visited us and redeemed us. He lifted up a horn of liberation for all humanity and he called us to serve him with holiness and justice all of our days. And whoever lives in the liberator is a new person, an ambassador of God's kingdom.

Reflect on the words of Paul: "[Christ's] purpose in dying for all was that men, while still in life, should cease to live for themselves, and should live for him who for their sake died and was raised to life. With us therefore worldly standards have ceased to count in our estimate of any man; even if once they counted in our understanding of Christ, they do so now no longer. When anyone is united to Christ, there is a new world; the old order has gone, and a new order has already begun" (2 Cor. 5:15–17).

This is the season to focus on the life of the church which bears the burden and joy of being the bearer of God's vision. It is an awesome responsibility. Often the church, aware of the vision, lives a life much like King Hezekiah. In Isaiah 39:1–10 is an account of this king who could think only of the present. To Isaiah's warning of the future he responded, "The word of the Lord which you have spoken is good; thinking to himself that peace and security would last out his lifetime" (Isa. 39:8).

How often the church has done the same? Nevertheless, the only justification for the church is that it lives for and bears witness to God's coming kingdom. In both word and deed the church is called to move out into the world by faith and with God signal the reality of God's vision. That may sound crazy but recall the words of Paul:

"Divine folly is wiser than the wisdom of man, and divine weakness stronger than man's strength. My brothers, think what sort of people you are, whom God has called. Few of you are men of wisdom, by any human standard; few are powerful or highly born. Yet, to shame the wise, God has chosen what the world counts folly, and to shame what is strong, God has chosen what the world counts weakness. He has chosen things low and contemptible, mere nothings, to overthrow the existing order" (1 Cor. 1:25–29).

Here is a revolutionary image of the church and a vision of its life which, while consistent with the Scriptures, is yet to be fully lived by those who claim to be followers of the crucified and risen Christ. Time marches on. The kingdom comes, and we are judged according to our faithfulness to God's vision. Let each of us and the church repent and return again to join God in the joy of kingdom-building.

The responsibility is great; it is ours. Recall the story of the feeding of the five thousand. Jesus and the disciples have had a long, hard day. They have spoken of the kingdom and cured those in need of healing. (Parenthetically, among those whom Jesus healed were lepers. It would be good for us to realize that in Jesus' day leprosy was seen not as a medical problem only, but as a social problem of exclusivism.) Well, the disciples wanted to be alone with their master. They suggested to Jesus that he send the people away to find food and lodging. And how does Jesus respond? "Give them something to eat yourselves," he exclaims (Luke 9:13). And they discovered that they could, and all were well-fed. Once again a sign of the kingdom's coming was revealed. And by whom? By those with faith who were bold enough to believe Jesus' good news that the kingdom had come. The church today is called to do likewise.

From Pentecost Through Kingdomtide

Almost half of the church year is known as kingdomtide. It is a good designation. The good news of the kingdom remains the central message of the Christian faith. The life of Christ, which we celebrate the other half of the year, recalls for us the imminence of God's kingdom. The church is called to live its life in and for God's kingdom-coming. During this season of the year it would be well for us to recall the character of God's kingdom.

Isaiah, after recounting how God the creator and ransomer had once saved his people from bondage and oppression by opening a path through the mighty waters, speaks for God:

Here and now I will do a new thing;
　　this moment it will break from the bud.
　　Can you not perceive it?
I will make a way even through the wilderness
　　and paths in the barren desert;
　　the wild beasts shall do me honour,
　　the wolf and the ostrich;
　for I will provide water in the wilderness
　　and rivers in the barren desert,
　　where my chosen people may drink.

(Isa. 43:19–20)

The vision of God is of cosmic newness. It must be understood in those terms. Recall the parable of Jesus: "No one tears a piece from a new cloak to patch an old one; if he does, he will have made a hole in the new cloak and the patch from the new will not match the old. Nor does anyone put new wine into old wine-skins; if he does the new wine will burst the skins, the wine will be wasted and the skins ruined. Fresh skins for new wine" (Luke 5:36–38). The world's ways and understandings are being replaced by God's ways and understandings. The new is being born and the old has no place.

And what is this new reality? God is bringing order and control, unity and peace, community and well-being, liberation, and justice into the world. Recall the story of the exodus and the song God's people sang after they had passed along the dry ground through the sea with the water making a wall for them.

I will sing to the Lord, for he has risen up in triumph;
the horse and his rider he has hurled into the sea.
　The Lord is my refuge and my defence,
　he has shown himself my deliverer.

(Exod. 15:1–2)

In thy constant love thou hast led the people

> whom thou didst ransom:
> thou hast guided them by thy strength
> to thy holy dwelling-place.
>
> (Exod. 15:13)

God has acted throughout history to bring the new into being, to realize his vision for all humanity. Recall also the Gospel story: "That day, in the evening, he said to them, 'Let us cross over to the other side of the lake.' So they left the crowd and took him with them in the boat where he had been sitting . . . . A heavy squall came on and the waves broke over the boat until it was all but swamped. Now he was in the stern asleep . . . they roused him and said, 'Master, we are sinking! Do you not care?' He awoke, rebuked the wind, and said to the sea, 'Hush! Be still!' The wind dropped and there was a dead calm. He said to them, 'Why are you such cowards? Have you no faith even now?' They were awestruck and said to one another, 'Who can this be? Even the wind and the sea obey him' " (Mark 4:35–41). In Christ, God uniquely acts to establish his kingdom. In him all things are made possible. God's vision can be—indeed is.

The kingdom of *shalom* comes where God's rule is known and honored. That is the covenant God made with Noah and his descendants. "I will make my covenant with you: never again shall all living creatures be destroyed by the waters of the flood, never again shall there be a flood to lay waste the earth" (Gen. 9:11).

That covenant is made new in Christ. "Through him God chose to reconcile the whole universe to himself, making peace through the shedding of his blood upon the cross— to reconcile all things, whether on earth or in heaven, through him alone" (Col. 1:20).

The covenant God establishes with all humanity points to the vision of *shalom,* to the kingdom of God, to life in this world characterized by:

Well-being

"I will give you rain at the proper time; the land shall yield its produce and the trees of the country-side their fruit. Threshing shall last till vintage and vintage till sowing; you shall eat your fill and live secure in your land" (Lev. 26:4–5).

Peace

"They shall beat their swords into mattocks and their spears into pruning-knives; nation shall not lift sword against nation nor ever again be trained for war" (Isa. 2:4).

Liberation

"They shall know that I am the Lord when I break the bars of their yokes and rescue them from those who have enslaved them. . . . I will give prosperity to their plantations; they shall never again be victims of famine in the land nor any longer bear the taunts of the nations" (Ezek. 34:27–29).

Justice

"The arrogant of heart and mind he has put to rout, he has brought down monarchs from their thrones, but the humble have been lifted high. The hungry he has satisfied with good things, the rich sent empty away" (Luke 1:51–53).

Unity

"Then I saw a new heaven and a new earth, for the first heaven and the first earth had vanished, and there was no longer any sea. I saw the holy city, new Jerusalem, coming down out of heaven from God, made ready like a bride adorned for her husband. I heard a loud voice proclaiming from the throne, 'Now at last God has his dwelling among men! He will dwell among them and they shall be his people, and God himself will be with them. He will wipe every tear from their eyes; there shall be an end to death, and to mourning and crying and pain; for the old order has passed away' " (Rev. 21:1–4).

For and in that vision the people of God are called to live. The church's educational ministry is given the responsibility to transmit that vision and its understandings so that the community of faith might be enabled to witness to that vision in word and deed.

Chapter Three

Hope
History Is Going Somewhere

It is one thing to dream dreams and long for visions. It is another to face reality. If we are to have hope, it must make sense of the dissonance between dreams and reality.

The vision of God's kingdom is beautiful and desirable, but we want to know if it is possible—or more important—is it probable? Reality raises serious questions for those who call us to live, let alone die, for God's kingdom. How much of a risk is a dream worth? Is there any assurance that our sacrifices will make any difference?

Christian hope boldly and confidently affirms that despite all evidence to the contrary, God's kingdom has come, is coming, and will come in all its glory; to live and to die for that vision makes good sense *and* is worth any price.

There will always be those who point out that this is difficult to believe. That's understandable. Alone, the question of hope is almost unresolvable. But the issue of hope is really the issue of God. If the God of the Old and New Testaments is real for us, then hope is reasonable. If God is not real, then hope is questionable. The question of hope is finally a matter of faith. It all depends upon the eyes through which we look at history.

The Difficulty of Faith

There are numerous reasons why God is not real to people in our day. The difficulty of faith involves our loss of a historical consciousness. We live in an ahistorical time. People long for history. (Consider the current interest in nostalgia.) But most people seem to lack a sense of history. Rather than being alive with meaning, history is most often understood as a meaningless collection of dates, names, and places.

Nevertheless, the Christian faith is founded upon a historicist perspective. God is the living God of history. God cannot be real and fully alive unless we perceive history as a realm of God's activity and living presence among us.

Too often, if we have told the story of God's activity in history, we have told that story as if it were a series of separate past events with a minimum of personal significance. For example, recall how God is said to have freed some Israelites from bondage in Egypt. How much more significant to recall how God once freed us from slavery and continues to free us. This, then, is the story of faith.

H. Richard Niebuhr distinguished between a living history and events in impersonal time; that is, between history lived and internalized, and history contemplated from the outside. To illustrate this he cited the *Cambridge Modern History*: "On July 4, 1776, Congress passed the resolution which made the colonies independent communities, issuing at the same time the well-known Declaration of Independence. We read in Lincoln's Gettysburg Address: 'Four-score and seven years ago our fathers brought forth on this continent a new nation, conceived in liberty and dedicated to the proposition that all men are created equal.'" Too often we have taught the history of our faith like the *Cambridge Modern History*. The result has been the atrophy of our historical consciousness, keeping us from experiencing the living God of history.

In religious education, if we continue to place our emphasis on doctrines, what persons ought to believe, and on the Bible as sacred literature to be memorized by verses, we will continue to prevent the development of a historicist perspective. We rather need to focus our educational efforts on story telling. We need to find ways to transmit the story of the faith as *our* story. From the earliest years in the context of a celebrating, faith community children, youth, and adults need to experience the faith story through song, dance, drama, and the visual arts. Educational efforts which teach *about* our history need to be avoided. It would be better to return to the fireside and supper table where we can dramatically retell the story of the mighty acts of God, and to our places of worship where we can celebrate our faith story. We need once again to become a storytelling people who use all the senses to recount our history of the living presence of God among us. We need to help persons regain their God-given ability to wonder and create; to dream, fantasize, imagine, and envision; to sing, paint, dance, and act. We need to enhance our natural capacity for ecstasy, for appreciating the new, the marvelous, the mysterious; to develop our God-given talent to express ourselves emotionally and non-verbally. Then God will be real and faith will be alive.

There is no better way to accomplish these ends than to once again become a people with a story. There was a time when we sang: "We've a story to tell to the nations." Let us sing it again! And let us share *the* story of our faith as *our* story for to know the story is to have faith and thus to have hope.

Called to Remember

The church is filled with discouraged, depressed, disheartened people. There is too little faith, too little hope, too little memory!

Christian faith calls us to remember that God acts in history, and because God acts, history is moving toward God's goal—God's kingdom. God's purposes are being worked out within history, among us. History appears to be out of control, but the Christian faith is founded upon the conviction that God is acting in our midst to bring the present chaos into order. Faith makes the unwavering affirmation that God is in control of history.

Listen to Paul's words to the church at Rome: "For I reckon that the sufferings we now endure bear no comparison with the splendour, as yet unrevealed, which is in store for us. . . . Up to the present, we know, the whole created universe groans in all its parts as if in the pangs of childbirth. Not only so, but even we, to whom the Spirit is given as firstfruits of the harvest to come, are groaning inwardly while we wait for God to make us his sons and set our whole body free. For we have been saved, though only in hope" (Rom 8:18, 22–24).

Paul admits that the claims of hope appear to be negated by contrary evidence. An "objective" look at our times will never reveal a sound basis for hope. But the Christian faith has never rested on rational, logical proof. Rather we turn to the Scriptures, to the story told by our foremothers and forefathers, for the assurances of hope. Christian faith's hope for tomorrow is grounded in our memory of yesterday. As "Fiddler on the Roof" reminds us, hope is founded on tradition.

Remember how our foreparents believed they were a people called by God. God had made a covenant with them about the future. And so they trusted. Of course they had problems to face. The denials of God's promises were real. No easy solutions, no Pollyanna attitudes or utopian daydreams occupied their thinking. But God, they were convinced, had entered history. It may be difficult to understand, but history is intentional and directional.

In Abraham we have the prototype of the faith-filled, hope-filled life. Recall how Abraham is called by God to leave the past behind and push into a new future, to become an adventurer in God's history. Abraham's future was not fated. He had a choice. He said "yes" by faith and lived for God and hence for humanity. When things seemed hopeless he remained strong in the faith that God would keep the promise. To expect great things of the future is at the very heart of the faith we bear. If God is the Lord of history, then surely God's purposes will be brought to conclusion. And so we hope!

It is a strange sort of hope, to be sure. Jeremiah tries to help us understand it. "To all the exiles whom I have carried off from Jerusalem to Babylon: Build houses and live in them; plant gardens and eat their produce. Marry wives and beget sons and daughters; take wives for your sons and give your daughters to husbands, so that they may bear sons and daughters and you may increase there and not dwindle away. Seek the welfare of any city to which I have carried you off, and pray to the Lord for it; on its welfare your welfare will depend" (Jer. 29:4–7).

Now that's not the message of hope we expect or desire. We don't want to wait patiently knowing that even our great grandchildren's children may not see the kingdom in all its glory. Nevertheless in the midst of the worst of times, Jeremiah performs a symbolic act; he buys a piece of land and thereby rejects both the illusion of those who expect a quick delivery from oppression and those who despair because they see no immediate future. As neither a prophet of revolution nor a priest of the status quo, Jeremiah calls for hope.

The hope to which our memory bears witness, therefore, is not a secular utopianism, though it is visionary. Our memory's hope is not based entirely upon human efforts, though it does not underestimate human nature and what it can be and do when put at the disposal of God. Our memory's hope is not overly optimistic, though it is never pessimistic.

Faith knows that this is God's world. God is acting in it. For those who share that faith there is always hope.

The Challenge

Remember how the psalmist exclaimed: "But the poor shall not always be unheeded, nor the hope of the destitute be always vain" (Ps. 9:18).

Hope is a message, especially for the outsider and for those who act as their advocates.

In speaking of God, the author of Job writes:

> He raises the lowly to the heights,
> the mourners are uplifted by victory;
> he frustrates the plots of the crafty,
> and they win no success,
> he traps the cunning in their craftiness,
> and the schemers' plans are thrown into confusion.
> In the daylight they run into darkness,
> and grope at midday as though it were night.
> He saves the destitute from their greed,
> and the needy from the grip of the strong;
> so the poor hope again,
> and the unjust are sickened.
>
> (Job 5:11–16)

God's hope is biased to the hurt, the captive, the left out. "To shame the wise, God has chosen what the world counts folly, and to shame what is strong, has chosen what the world counts weakness. He has chosen things low and contemptible, mere nothings, to overthrow the existing order" (1 Cor. 1:28). No, it is not more human to be low and despised; to the contrary, that is why God is struggling with them and for them in their quest for human life.

Our loss of hope signals our loss of God. And our loss of God is due to our inability or refusal to see where God is at work in the world. Only if we identify with the "have nots," and their quest for abundant life, can we regain a sense of God's action in history.

To live in the hope of the gospel is to search for where

God is acting in the world and to join God in those actions. One way the gospel suggests that we do this is to listen attentively to the cries and aspirations of the marginal peoples among us. In their voices we can discern the voice of God. In their struggles for liberation and justice we can see the activity of God. To live in the gospel's hope we need to identify with the outsiders and risk joining them in their liberating actions.

Jesus was not absorbed in the moral philosophical question, What ought I to do? Rather, his will was directed toward what God was doing and his question was, How am I to respond and will God's will? To share the faith of Jesus is to recognize that God is acting in history on behalf of persons, institutions, and nations.

Hope founded in Christ has no alternative but to engage in actions which challenge the evils of society—poverty, ignorance, disease, oppression, injustice, war, and prejudice—and to create more human alternatives in line with God's will. If we are to live by hope there are some things the church can and indeed must do.

I'll name a few: The church is called to stop contributing to our social ills. The church is called to take a stand on social issues. The church is called to raise a prophetic voice against injustice. The church is called to take positive action on behalf of liberation. The church is called to influence public opinion. The church is called to join with others working for social justice. The church is called to identify with and become the advocate of the outsider. The church is called to eliminate the chasm between personal and social religion. (Why don't we turn the current enthusiasm for the Holy Spirit—long overdue—into a concern for the manifestation of the works of the Holy Spirit?) The church is called to respond to people's hunger for spiritual life by relating worship and prayer to social action—both together are the work (liturgy) of the community of faith.

A number of years ago I was working with a group of youth in a local church. We were struggling with the relationship between worship and the Christian life. The offering, as we knew it, presented us with numerous problems. One of our group pointed to the church's yearly offering for racial justice and said, "That is my father's guilt money, and I'll tell you one thing, he prays that it will not be spent here in our town." Another chimed in, "If they ever did put that money to work in overcoming prejudice and injustice in our town my parents would stop their giving." (This, by the way, was in a church that had set a record for financial contributions to racial justice.) As we reflected on the meaning of our offering we arrived at this understanding: The offering is a symbolic act of a community of faith in response to the gospel, indicating before God our intention to act. With that understanding in mind we tried to think of ways we could turn our racial justice offering into a Christian act. Someone suggested that we send out fair-housing pledge cards to all our members. Then during the offering have a procession so that each member could bring forward his or her signed card and place it on the altar. That would be a real offering, we concluded. And so it would. But a church can only make an offering such as that if it lives by and for the hope of the gospel.

The gospel's hope implies that God brings in the kingdom, but in a radical sense it also affirms that we build it. The shape, character, and time of its coming is in God's hands, but we are to be the building stones upon which the master builder constructs the kingdom and without which it could not exist.

We are called to seek after, pray for, and work in God's kingdom-coming. It is our role to be the good ground in which the seed of the sower can grow and bring forth much fruit. God's kingdom is present where God's will is accepted and obeyed. We live in that kingdom by giving God our loyalty and our wills. We pray: God's kingdom come and God's will be done on earth. To pray that prayer is to identify with the "have nots," advocating their cause, and working for justice, liberation, peace, well-being and the unity of all humanity. And the answer to our prayer is hope for the struggle.

Like our forefathers and foremothers who labored with God in kingdom-building, we cannot expect to complete the task, but neither can we refrain from making our own contribution.

We are free to say yes or no to the call of God mediated through the events of history. Depending upon our response, history moves humanity toward fulfillment or diverts humanity from its proper goal. History is a dialogue between ourselves and God. God never gives up; God continues to move the universe toward fulfillment by calling us to a vision and eliciting from us an affirmative response and corresponding action. To respond to God's call is to live in faith. And to live in faith is to know hope. All things are possible when our wills and God's will unite in historical action. That is the joyful message of our Christian tradition.

Trials and Tribulations

But what should we make of the discouragement and sometimes suffering which accompany our abortive efforts and defeats? Hear these words carefully:

"Hard-pressed on every side, we are never hemmed in; bewildered, we are never at our wits' end; hunted, we are never abandoned to our fate; struck down, we are not left to die. Wherever we go we carry death with us in our body, the death that Jesus died, that in this body also life may reveal itself, the life that Jesus lives. For continually, while still alive, we are being surrendered into the hands of death, for Jesus' sake, so that the life of Jesus also may be revealed in this mortal body of ours" (2 Cor. 4:8–11).

I would like to testify that Paul's witness is true. We can endure reversals and failures of all kinds. Why? Because, through the eyes of faith we are able to see positive value in them. Hear Paul again: "If God is on our side, who is against us?" (Rom. 8:31).

> For I am convinced that there is nothing in death or
> life, in the realm of spirits or superhuman powers, in
> the world as it is or the world as it shall be, in the
> forces of the universe, in heights or depths—nothing
> in all creation that can separate us from the love of
> God in Christ Jesus our Lord (Rom. 8:38–39).

In this faith resides invincible hope. The struggle against
the ultimately defeated principalities and powers—the social,
economic, and political forces of this world—is worthwhile,
even if each attempt appears to be more futile than the last.
In our lifetime it is not final victory, but faithful striving
that has ultimate meaning and purpose. To be sustained by
such faith is to possess abundant hope.

To live in the hope of the gospel is to believe that the
struggle with the principalities and powers is not futile. The
task may be massive and the resistance great, but we are
motivated by faith in God. In God there is hope for the
building of a new age. Perhaps only those who risk joining
God in the continuing transformation of the world can know
it.

> . . . those who look to the Lord will win new strength,
> they will grow wings like eagles;
> they will run and not be weary,
> they will march on and never grow faint.
>
> (Isa. 40:31)

Hope reaches beyond the possibilities of our imaginations
and witnesses to the possibility of God. In the gospel, hope
is kindled anew. In the good news of the kingdom's coming
is hope beyond hope. Such hope is the power to move mountains; it is faith in the impossible possibility of God.

All too frequently we have based our hope on either what
we can accomplish or on what God will accomplish alone.
Such actions and non-actions misunderstand the nature of
God's kingdom-coming. In the gospel faith, neither we nor

God alone builds the kingdom. Rather God works in and through persons and historical groups. Only insofar as we make a positive response to God's actions and live for the kingdom will God bring in the kingdom. Christian hope is knowing that we are never alone if we will God's will. Christian hope is knowing that to act with God is to make a difference in the world.

Christian hope prevents us from quitting when an awareness of the immensity and complexity of the problem faces us. Christian hope eliminates our doubts about the significance of our efforts. Of course, the problems our world faces are legion. At best we can only address small aspects of a few problems. But our feeble effort can make a difference. How?

Let me share this story about a solitary action by a social scientist who was studying the culture of a fishing village in the West Indies. The men, he found, worked in teams of eight. Together each group owned and operated a fishing boat. Unity, cooperation, and harmony typified this closely knit community. He did notice, however, that each day they dragged their heavy boats up on the shore. It was a painful process and the scars of injury were borne for life. In compassion, he suggested that they use a motor and construct a winch to pull their boats up on the shore. They did. It was a small simple change, but it resulted in the destruction of their corporate life. The men began to fight; community evaporated, and the society began to come apart. Why? Because that one seemingly insignificant change eliminated their dependence upon one another.

One single action can make a great difference. You and I do make a difference in this world. That is not the issue. The issue is whether or not our influence is positive, that is, whether or not it is consistent with God's will.

What God requires is faithful actions. Insofar as our actions in society correspond to God's intentions, it matters little how important they seem to us. They are significant for God's kingdom-building.

Even our failings, faith informs us, do not have to result in hopelessness. I have a symbol of that truth in my office. Once I was a consultant to the vice president of children's television at NBC. I took the job because I intended to reform children's television. One of my reforms was "Take a Giant Step," a youth show on values. It folded after a couple of years. Other attempts at reform also died. Some friends at NBC gave me a present. They created a *Time* magazine "Man of the Year" cover with my picture on it. Jokingly, they told me it was to be a reminder of the impossibility of change. It is now a different sort of reminder—the continuing demand to keep hoping and striving for change. With faith in God, change is possible. I still believe that. I will continue to commit my life to social change. I will never feel defeated. My hope is in God.

Hope lives in the confidence that new possibilities for life exist, that our present social systems and patterns of life are not fated to be. Such Christian hope does not remain passive, it does not sit and wait. Hope is active. It motivates us to act on behalf of our understanding of God's purposes, intentions, and desires. Nevertheless, this orientation, which is Christian hope in action, does not live in a next week or next century future. The future for which we hope and act is always an approaching future. This means, nothing that happens or does not happen within our lifetime can count against the future—God's future.

Never Despair

The gospel faith is charged with hope; it is expectant and anticipatory. The apostles, as witnesses to an event, became bearers of an announcement which testified to the shattering of the old order. They declared that God had acted and the kingdom of God had arrived—a new era had begun, a new stage in human history consistent with the past actions of God.

The kingdom of God is here and not here—it is in process. A new covenant is offered; a new response demanded. Hope is at its center. We are called to live in and for the kingdom's coming and not expect that it will be built to completion in our time or by our hands alone. Nevertheless, the possibility of constructing a truly human future is before us. And we can in mysterious ways contribute to its realization.

Surely no political, social, or economic revolution can be identified with God's kingdom. We cannot put our hope in the destruction of the old. Neither can we put our hope in any particular positive human accomplishment. The reforms of today will always become the grounds for reform tomorrow. Indeed, often the reforms of yesterday become the oppressions of today. Consider the great educational reforms of the nineteenth century. Confronted by an educational system which ignored the talents, abilities, and the potential of individual students, a means of measuring a person's intellectual ability was constructed. School systems adopted these tests to help them judge the best means of education for each student. Today these same IQ tests have become an instance of oppression. Constructed by and for white middle-class students they have been proven to be inadequate for measuring the potential of Black, Chicano, and first American students. Using the results of these tests continues to hurt minority students. The reform of testing for potential and intelligence needs to be called into question. Yesterday's reform must now be reformed.

For some this is a depressing revelation. Not for me. I never assume that any reform I commit myself to is a reform for all times. We can never anticipate all the consequences of our actions. Yet, to wait until we are confident a reform is guaranteed to produce only good results, is to avoid all action. Of course we ought to consider consequences before we act, but let no one ever believe that they can be faultless in that responsibility. Reforms by their very nature tend to be reactionary. We reform acknowledged evils by trying to imagine and create a corresponding good. Due to the limitations of human nature, and we could add human sin, we will never produce the perfect solution to any problem. In time we will need to reform our reforms. But do not despair. What is most important is that while realizing our limitations, we boldly assume the risk and act as we believe God's will demands.

The Christian is called to move from reform to reform always judging the products of his or her last reform, imagining better alternatives and risking new solutions. The meaning in the life of continual reform is found in the gospel's hope. It is the life of the faithful pilgrim in exile. Having seen the kingdom we live outside its gates singing a song of hope in a foreign land (Psalm 137).

To live in hope is to believe that God's kingdom-coming will be realized in God's good time, and that our fumbling efforts in faith will, in strange and mysterious ways, contribute to its coming. Encompassed by a host of witnesses within the historic community of faith we react and act in confidence that our lives make a difference in the eternal plan of God.

This hope makes it possible for us to sing and dance even in evil days. Daily we can celebrate the victory party of the people of God, the Eucharist, and go forth again to struggle with the principalities and powers. Surely with hope there is no reason to bemoan being called to live between the times.

A Testimony to Faith

A moving report from an imprisoned Latin American pastor was shared at the Fifth Assembly of the World Council of Churches' meeting in Nairobi. It concerned an Easter spent in prison. The charge: witnessing to the demands of the Christian faith through social action.

What has the resurrection of Christ to say to political prisoners who have no idea what tomorrow will bring and whose very lives are precariously uncertain? In this case the prisoners had been forbidden to worship. Yet without bread or wine, they celebrated a memorable Easter communion.

While the non-Christians talked quietly so the guards would not notice, the Christians, we were told, huddled together. The pastor began: "This meal, in which we take part, reminds us of the prison, the torture, the death, and the final victory of the resurrection of Jesus Christ. He asked us to remember Him by repeating this action in the spirit of fellowship. The bread which we do not have today, but which is present in the spirit of Jesus Christ, is the body which he gave for humanity. The fact that we have none represents very well the lack of bread in the hunger of so many millions of human beings. When Christ distributed it among his disciples, or when he fed the people, he revealed the will of God that all should have bread. The wine which we do not have today is His blood, present in the light of our faith. Christ poured it out for us to move us toward freedom, in the long march for justice. God made all persons of one blood. The blood of Christ represents our dream of the unified humanity, of a just society without difference of race or class."

Then the reporter told of a man about sixty, whose daughter had died fighting with the guerrillas. He said, "I think this communion means that our dead are alive. They have given their bodies and their blood making Christ's sacrifice their own. I believe in the resurrection of our dead and I feel their presence among us."

There was silence and the pastor continued. "This communion is not only a communion between us here, but a communion with all of our brothers and sisters in the church who are outside, not only those who live, but those who have already died, but still more it is a communion with those who will come after us and who will be faithful to Jesus Christ." He then is said to have held out his empty hand to each person, placing his hand over their open hands and together they boldly exclaimed, "Take, eat, this is my body which is given for you, do this in remembrance of me." Then they repeated together, "Take, drink, this is the blood of Christ which was shed to seal the new covenant of God with humanity. Let us give thanks, sure that Christ is here with us, strengthening us!" They raised their hands to their mouths and received the body and blood of Christ. And after sharing the kiss of peace, they returned to their prison life with new hope.

The witness of hope! It is powerful and convincing. It is a story lived and told by our forefathers and foremothers; it is a story shared in word and deed among the faithful of every age.

But how well do we who have been baptized and confirmed in that same faith live hope? Will our children understand that it is worthwhile to suffer and die for justice? What sort of hope will they know? Will it motivate them to do God's will without counting the cost or anticipating the benefits?

Do we live by, in, and for the gospel's hope? What do our churches' budgets reveal about our hope? How does our worship generate hope and stimulate hopeful action in the world? Is the gospel's hope revealed through the actions of our community of faith in society? Do those who participate in our churches' life experience hope?

The questions could go on. Their answers will be found in an examination of our corporate life, not in our church school lessons. Our actions speak louder than our words. If Christian hope is to be transmitted and understood, it must be experienced in a learning and witnessing community of memory and faith. Christian education needs to help us evaluate and judge our lives as communities of faith and thereby facilitate our becoming communities of hope.

Without hope we are dead. With hope all things are possible. With hope we are empowered to act with God. With hope we are willing to give our lives for the outsider, aware that the only reward is in knowing we have been faithful. With hope we are able to live without evidence of the kingdom's coming and still risk our lives on its behalf. With hope, living for visions makes sense. With hope our deepest concern is not progress, but faithfulness to the will of God. With hope the frustrating, sometimes depressing struggle for social change gains meaning. With hope we have power greater than the principalities and powers against which we struggle. With hope we are enabled to be a pilgrim people in an evil land united with the outsider in the struggle for justice, liberation, unity, community, peace, and well-being.

This hope can be ours. In the memory of our tradition lies its roots. Through life in a community of faith it is nurtured. By an act of faith it comes to life within us. And it blossoms and grows as we join with others in doing God's Word in the world.

Chapter Four

Power
Called to Responsibility

Fine, you say, God's vision is desirable. When owned, it establishes goals and therefore meaning and purpose for individual and corporate life. Hope makes sense out of God's vision in the world of reality. Because we have hope, it is worth risking our lives for that vision. But, is there anything practical we humans—alone or together—can do? Do we have any power to contribute to God's kingdom-building? Can we make any real difference in the world? How can the church become an instrument of God's historical action? What is it to will God's will and assume responsible power? Until we resolve these questions about power, vision and hope remain somewhat irrelevant to daily life in this world.

To begin, we have to admit that the word "power" is not popular in the church. Neither is "politics" or "social action." Recently I explored the beliefs of some one hundred active adult church members in a Southern county. This is what I discovered:

Visions are understood as other-worldly promises. Hope is trust that God will reward you in heaven. Those who have done well in this world have an obligation to aid the unfortunate. But of greatest value is the saving of souls for eternity.

These adults said that they learned these beliefs in their Sunday schools. I don't doubt it, but I could not find these ideas in the printed curriculum their teachers used. It was simply a part of the hidden curriculum of their churches. They learned these beliefs by going to church and by observing the church's life. Their understanding of "power" corresponded with their other beliefs. Power was something other people possessed—people in the news, people in big cities, people in important places, especially government. God had the greatest power, but God's power was not in this world. The church didn't have power. Indeed that was good, for the church was not supposed to have power. Politics was necessary but it had nothing to do with religion. The church was to stay out of politics. Social action was not Christian. The church's business was to save souls for life with God and Jesus in heaven.

Well, I do not doubt that they learned all that in church nor do I doubt that they read all that *into* the Bible. What concerns me is this: What can we do to help individuals as persons of power and the church as a community of power to comprehend the historic Christian understanding of its responsible use in the world?

Power and the Tradition

To begin, it may be helpful to reflect on Scripture. Power, social action, and change are all there. That is, if we have the eyes of faith to see it. Recall Jesus' words spoken to the apostles after his resurrection. "You will receive power when the Holy Spirit comes upon you; and you will bear witness for me" (Acts 1:8). The power we possess is a gift of the Spirit; it is to be used to witness in word and deed to the good news of the kingdom's coming. The Scriptures are quite clear—change in society and history are the intention of God. Throughout the Old and New Testaments God is most often understood as an agent of social change in history. To witness to God is to witness with God. So it was that "Stephen, who was full of grace and power, began to work great miracles and signs among the people" (Acts 6:8). And what were these signs, but acts demonstrating the kingdom's coming. We, like Stephen, are to do the same. So is the church. As Paul reminds the church in Corinth, "The kingdom of God is not a matter of talk, but of power" (1 Cor. 4:20). God does not want listeners *to* the Word or speakers *for* the Word. God desires DOERS of the Word. As apostles sent by the living God of history, we are to act out our faith in the world—individually and corporately. The church, the body of Christ, is to be a missionary church, a church that acts with God in mission to transform the world into the kingdom of our Lord and Savior Jesus Christ.

The church, bold enough to claim Christ as her Lord, is judged by how well she follows God's purposes and actions: namely, to engage in the responsible use of power so that the redemptive purpose of God in the liberation and unification of all people in justice and love is accomplished.

The demand to love God and neighbor has been accepted as normative, but the church has not always acted accordingly. How can we love God if we are not engaged in social action on behalf of the kingdom's coming? How can we love our neighbor if we do not attack and reform those systemic social structures that prevent our neighbor from receiving the benefits and blessings of God's kingdom?

Recall that the mission of the "seventy-two" sent by Jesus (Luke 10:1–24) is directed not only to individuals but to whole towns. Jesus' message "the kingdom of God has come close to you" (Luke 10:9), which they were to announce, was aimed at changing the basic structures of society. Remember that Jesus demanded the rich ruler to "sell everything you have and distribute to the poor" (Luke 18:22). And it was Paul who reminded the church at Ephesus that their struggle "is not against human foes, but against cosmic powers, against the authorities and potentates of this dark world" (Eph. 6:12).

The fundamental motive of Jesus' ministry was founded upon his sense of the purpose of God for the world and of God's will for him to accomplish that purpose. He was absolutely convinced that God is at work in the world establishing a kingdom of peace, unity, justice, well-being, community, and liberation where all people may live together in obedience to God's will. Knowing that he would not live to see the consummation of God's rule, Jesus gathered together disciples commissioning them to continue his mission of announcing and ushering in the rule of God by word and deed.

James, "a servant of God and the Lord Jesus Christ," remembered this commission and in a letter to the churches explained to them that the Christian faith was to be practical.

James's letter begins by pointing to the importance of faith. The doubter, he writes, is like a heaving sea ruffled by the wind. Without faith we can never keep a steady course. Up to this point there is easy agreement. Then he makes his central point.

"My brothers, what use is it for a man to say he has faith when he does nothing to show it? Can that faith save him? Suppose a brother or a sister is in rags with not enough food for the day, and one of you says, 'Good luck to you, keep yourselves warm, and have plenty to eat,' but does nothing to supply their bodily needs, what is the good of that? So with faith; if it does not lead to action, it is in itself a lifeless thing" (James 2:14–17).

Following these biting words on faith and deeds, James reiterates the gospel message of justice and mercy. He reminds us once again that the "have nots"—those who are impotent, in hunger, poverty, ignorance, disease, and despair—will be lifted up .That is God's will! And the "haves"— those with potency, money, health, security, food, position, and luxury and the "have-some-but-want-a-little-more's" who are to be included with the "haves"—will be brought low. Indeed he makes a point of telling the "haves" and those on their way to becoming "haves" that they had better weep and

wail over their fate, for God's will is that they humble themselves in repentant action by seeking the good of the "have
nots."

That is a revolutionary, social, political, economic message
for the church and it obviously deals with power and action
and social change. Of course, other less radical, other-worldly,
individualistic thoughts can be read into it, but not if the
total message of the Scriptures (God's Word) is read and
heard with the eyes and the ears of faith in Jesus Christ.

No faith is real that is not accompanied by deeds. Our
faith is always at work in our actions. By our deeds we prove
our faith. This is true for persons; it is true for the church.
Social action, power, and social change are words that belong
with the gospel and the kingdom of God.

Definitions and Understandings

Power is an essential life force. Without power we cannot
be human. Without using power responsibly we cannot be
the church of Jesus Christ.

God has power. Who among us would deny that? Because
we are created in God's image, we have power also. To deny
our power is to deny our inheritance; and to deny our
parentage is to deny God. Power is of God's essence. It is
God's gift to all of us at creation. Power can be rejected or
accepted. It can be used for good or evil; it cannot be denied.
But what is it?

Power, as I will be using the word, *is the ability, right,
and responsibility to react and act to influence.*

Let me explain this definition.

ABILITY

To possess the ability to do something is to have the
necessary capacities, skills, and talents. It means you can,
you are able. Freedom is crucial. There are those in the
world who lack capacity because they do not have freedom.
Some have been brought up to be dependent upon the
decisions of someone else. For others, social structures do

not permit or encourage them to make their own decisions. To lack freedom is to be oppressed. Whether it is an internal or external oppression, it is oppression just the same. No one is liberated or has capacity unless he or she is freed from absolute dependence upon others.

Ability also implies skills or talents. Skills are learned. Talents are God-given abilities that we possess at birth, but which need to be nurtured into actualization. Particular individual skills and talents must be taught and nurtured if we are to be free and hence able. To have been denied these capacities for freedom is to be in need of liberation. The end of liberation is to make us able!

RIGHTS AND RESPONSIBILITIES

Power not only implies abilities, but rights and responsibilities. "You, my friends, were called to be free men" (Gal. 5:13), wrote Paul. Power is a God-given right which no one should be denied. Because that is true, power is also an obligation. To be a child of God, a faithful citizen in God's world, is to assume responsibility for the power that is given us by God at birth. When the church denies or neglects its gift of power, it denies its Lord. The church cannot be faithful and ignore power. Power is an individual and social birthright. It must be used responsibly.

TO REACT TO INFLUENCE

To react is to respond freely to outside influences. Influence is all about us and always will be. Insofar as we live in the world, we live with influence. Some is good and some is not. The environment in which we live, the people we meet, the organizations to which we belong, the institutions within which we work and upon which we depend, all attempt consciously and unconsciously to influence us. To have power is to possess the ability, right, and responsibility to freely accept or reject that influence. As free persons in Christ, we are not to let ourselves be overly influenced by the way things are or the way things are presently done. We are called to judge, according to God's standards, the legitimacy of any and all outside influence upon either ourselves or others. Our ultimate authority is God. All other authorities are to be called into question and listened to only because their moral example, personhood, or wisdom corresponds to God's will, desires, and wisdom.

TO ACT TO INFLUENCE

As children of God—the God who acts in history on behalf of the kingdom's coming—we are responsible to make decisions and act with God. Because we live in a social world, social action is the obligation and responsibility we share. What are we as believers in Christ and members of his church to do? We are to be an influence on the world. We are to be the salt of the earth. We are not to force our will and ways on others, thereby taking away their freedom, but we are called to influence. We are required to strive for social change in the world, change which is in harmony with God's will. We are to act in society in ways that witness to God's kingdom-coming. The church cannot be the body of Christ unless it assumes responsible power in society, unless it seeks to influence.

Perceptions and Power

In a sense we all live in three worlds—a personal world, an interpersonal world, and a social world.

Our *personal world* is the world of our immediate family or that small group of significant others who assume the functions of family in our lives.

Our *interpersonal world* is the world of close meaningful relationships founded upon shared values, behaviors, and understandings. Our interpersonal world is the world of *voluntary associations*. The congregation (community of faith) to which we belong is, or ought to be, an example. Others are: the American Association of University Women; the League of Women Voters; The National Education Association; the American Bar Association; the American

Medical Association; the Civil Liberties Union; the Farm
Workers' Union; the Rotary Club, etc.

Our *social world* is the world of impersonal institutions
and organizations which daily affect our lives directly, indirectly, or subtly. We live in a society of organizations. They
pervade every aspect of our lives, day and night. There are
all sorts: business (General Motors, Avon Products); media
(NBC, the *Washington Post*); labor (AFL-CIO); educational (Ohio State University, the University of Texas school
system); medical-health (Blue Cross-Blue Shield, Parke-Davis
Pharmaceutical); social welfare (Veterans Administration);
government-political (HEW, Congress); criminal justice (Office of the Attorney General, the Supreme Court), and
religious (United Methodist Church, Southern Baptist
Convention).

We are shaped by these organizations and institutions.
They influence us directly by the way they meet or fail to
meet the needs of people. No institution has a right to exist
in a society for the profit motive alone. Because they have a
direct effect upon people they have a responsibility to them.
Organizations and institutions either facilitate or impede,
serve or frustrate our daily needs. They largely determine our
health care, educational possibilities, sanitation services,
police protection, employment and leisure opportunities.

Organizations and institutions also indirectly affect us.
When U.S. Steel raises the prices of steel or the government
raises the tax on oil, every aspect of people's lives all around
the world are affected.

Also important are the subtle influences organizations and
institutions have on our values and life-styles. Consider the
advertisements on TV as just one example.

We ought not to ignore the social world. But we do. It
seems that most people feel more at home in the world of
personal and interpersonal relationships. For some strange,
or perhaps not so strange reason, we understand the Christian life only in terms of our personal and interpersonal

worlds. We tend to leave the social world of organizations and institutions outside our preview. To do so is irresponsible and faithless.

Consider, for a moment, three faith responses to a common situation. There is a sharp curve in a road. Without fail, that curve is a major contributing cause to a daily accident. People and property are injured. From the perspective of a personal world-view, faith demands that we volunteer to be available to help the victims of the accidents and their families in any way possible.

From an interpersonal perspective, faith demands a more satisfactory response. We find that we cannot always be present to lend a hand, often we do not know what to do, and when we know what needs to be done we find we lack the necessary skills to do it. In response, through our church, or another voluntary association, we raise money to build a rescue and community service facility near the site of the accidents and we fund a few professionals to assume responsibility. By so doing, we provide better, more efficient care for those victimized by the curve.

The church, through the years, has used both the personal and interpersonal perspective for addressing human need. Consider the needs of the poor. A good example of a personal response is food baskets at Thanksgiving and toys at Christmas. An example of an interpersonal response is leadership in the United Fund or support of a school breakfast-lunch program. We have a pretty good record in personal and social services. But our record in social action is quite inadequate.

Faced by our same curve in the road, a reasonable faith response from a social world perspective is to organize pressure on the town government to straighten the road. In response to our example of poverty, a reasonable faith response is to organize pressure on government to legislate for a guaranteed annual income. My conviction is simply that the gospel of God's kingdom-coming makes the social world perspective central. And therefore, social action—the responsible use of power—is crucial to the church's life and mission.

If we live in a world that is shaped by organizations and institutions, we as Christians have an obligation to make and keep them just and humane. The way we do that is through continual social judgment and pressure, which implies social action. It ought to be clear to us that if God's vision for the world is to be realized for all peoples and the message of hope is to have meaning to the oppressed, we need to assume responsibility for the use of power in society.

The Church and Power

Our power is directly related to the groups, the voluntary associations to which we belong. By ourselves we may have limited personal and interpersonal power but we have no social power. Indeed, without a supportive group, all power is soon diminished or eliminated. Consider the issue of influence. I used to conduct workshops for individual ministers or lay persons. Often they were helped to gain a heightened awareness of the crucial issues that face our society; they were aided in learning skills in social analysis and planning; they were equipped and stimulated for action. On occasion someone described their experience as having been to the top of a mountain. Then, they returned home to the church from which they had come. No one wanted to hear about their mountaintop experience. No one shared their new understandings and behaviors. Soon they lost their motivation to act and returned to their old ways (ways consistent with their group) of thinking and behaving. Or in frustration and sometimes anger, they left the church and sought another group of persons like themselves. If they could not find a community to affirm, share and support them, they, in time, lost their newly acquired ways of thinking and behaving.

All power is dependent upon belonging to a group which shares our understandings and goals. A friend of mine used to shock some people by saying that when he moved to a new community he went church-hunting. When he visited a church he would ask the minister and lay leaders to share with him their short and long range goals. Most didn't even understand his question. A few who did were upset when he told them that he would have to look elsewhere because they were not consistent with his own. Only when he found a congregation that shared his understandings and goals and could demonstrate by their program and budget that they were truly committed to them would he seek to join in their life. What he knew was this: if he was to have power he needed a church that shared his commitments and was involved in corresponding action.

While few of us consciously go through such a procedure, many of us do so unconsciously. That is why we are known by our groups. Tell me the groups you belong to and I will tell you what you believe and how you are most likely to act. Why? Because we all seek groups that support our ways and understandings. And we behave in ways these groups approve and encourage.

Few of us are exclusively members of a church. We are often members of numerous interpersonal communities or voluntary associations. To have social power we are required to be active in voluntary associations. Only groups that assert power in the world of institutions and organizations can effect social change. We ought, as Christians, to engage in social action through the various associations to which we belong. We must be responsible for the gift of power which God grants us all as a birthright.

The church should be equipping, encouraging, and supporting us for this task. There is a depressing amount of evidence, however, that the religious beliefs of persons have little influence on their social lives. This is true, I believe, because the church has, to a great extent, forfeited its obligation to engage in social action. Only if our faith community is engaged in social action will we learn to use our faith in other voluntary associations. If the church does not assume power in the secular world, persons will not see the relationship of faith to life in institutions and organizations.

Remember Paul's advice: "Adapt yourselves no longer to the pattern of this present world, but let your minds be remade and your whole nature thus transformed. Then you will be able to discern the will of God and to know what is good, acceptable, and perfect" (Rom. 12:2).

We are called, as followers of the crucified and risen Christ, to be loving critics in the world of institutions and organizations. It is important to affirm and support our institutions and organizations when they are responding to the needs of humanity. It is equally important to assert a prophetic judgment upon them when they are not. In either case our obligation is clear. We are responsible to act within self-conscious, goal-oriented voluntary associations (especially the church) to make the institutions and organizations of society more just and humane. That is what it means to possess responsible social power.

Many of us, as children, were brought up with idealized views of the American Way of Life and its social institutions. Few of us were taught the skills necessary for social change. As adults we are confronted with mounting social problems. Various options are open to us. We can find a wailing wall and cry for ourselves and the world—a cop-out. We can go mad and support the rhetoric of violent social revolution. We can ignore the seriousness of our situation, talk ourselves into this being the best of all possible worlds and strive to benefit from it as much as possible. We can catch a vision, join with others who share that vision, learn social change skills, organize, assert power, and use it responsibly for democratic social change. Or we can admit we face serious problems and spend our time studying and talking about them until they overwhelm us.

Since I fear that the church is most apt to make this latter response, I would like to share a tragically amusing story, "Pigs is Pigs," by Ellis Butler. The main character is the manager of a railway station where it costs more to ship farm animals than domestic pets. A customer brings in two pigs and claims they are pets, and therefore would like the cheaper price. The station manager pages through his book of regulations but can find no answer to the problem. All the while, the pigs are multiplying. Finally the pigs win the day and overrun the station while the manager is left at his desk still searching for a solution to the problem of the pigs.

As Edmund Burke once said, "The only thing necessary for the triumph of evil is for good men to do nothing." We cannot wait for surety before we act, unless we want to invite calamity.

Foundations for Power

As Christians we are called to be persons of love, power, and justice. Justice is the end for which we are to live. Love is the means by which we are to strive for justice. Power makes love seeking justice possible. However, to be persons of power we need to possess particular qualities and we need to belong to communities with particular qualities.

Social change is inhibited by lost vision and hope, by reluctance to depart from the known, by indifference to the needs of others, by fear and insecurity, by laziness, by a lack of imagination, curiosity and creativity, by humorlessness, and by irresponsible patience.

Concern for others, imagination, curiosity, creativity, and a sense of humor are God-given qualities. Motivation, hope, security, trust, urgency, and the willingness to face the unknown are gifts of faith. Of course both these God-given qualities and gifts of faith need to be nurtured, transmitted, and sustained, but all are possible for each of us.

Discovery and the imagination are wonders of life. Creativity is an astounding gift; curiosity a blessing. Too few of us adults are filled with questions and challenges. Children are! That is why we are to become as children. To be a person of power we need to recover the naturalness of asking: Is that true? Is that the way things have to be? Is that the best way? We will never find a better way until we learn to question our present ways; curiosity leads to discovery.

Dis-cover. When we create, we uncover what is before us, we reveal something that was there all along but which we did not previously see. In a block of stone is the creation of the sculpture, within a scale of notes is a symphony, and within our fallen world is the kingdom of God. We will never discover God in our midst without an open mind— a mind that is always entertaining new notions and possibilities to the givens of life. Without imagination we cannot dream the impossible dream. Without inner directedness we cannot take up our cross and follow after Jesus.

Most revelatory and creative acts are achieved in the face of common sense and conventional wisdom. When Columbus took off for the East via the West it must have appeared a ludicrous act to most people, for any idiot *could* see that the world was flat. Each of us needs to learn to remove the blinders from our eyes which prevent us from finding creative new solutions to our social problems. All of us have the same God-given ability as the famous young mathematician Gauss. Remember how one day he asked his class to find the sum of $1+2+3+4+5+6+7+8+9+10$. He discovered that most of his students took each number as it came in sequence from left to right and added them together. It was a somewhat slow, tedious operation. Gauss took one look at the same problem and discovered another, better way. He immediately saw that there were non-sequential relations: $1 + 10 = 11$, so does $2 + 9$, $3 + 8$, etc., making five pairs of 11 for a total of 55. Regretfully this talent to discover the new has been drained off by our being told, as children, there is a "right" way to do things and that this is the way things "are." The beautiful truth is, however, that we can learn again to use our atrophied God-given talents.

It is instructive to observe the creative process at work.

Take the artist as an example. Most often he or she begins with some sort of internal or external conflict. Because no one can live with unresolved conflict the artist attempts to resolve it by envisioning a number of possible alternatives (sketches they are called). Then with a series of self-created criteria for judgment, the artist evaluates each and chooses the one which appears best. Finally a statement is made (the painting). Then something interesting occurs. The artist finds him or herself once again in conflict. With the old conflict resolved, a new one has emerged. And so the creative process continues.

That model of creativity suggests a helpful model for the responsible use of power. Try it. Become aware. Sense the injustice and oppression around you. Let yourself be consumed by the conflict between what is and what ought to be—justice and liberation. Imagine the great variety of ways this dissonance can be overcome. Use the gospel's criteria of love to judge your alternatives. (Remember that love does not mean to like a person, it means to seek his or her good. We are not commanded to like our neighbors, but to be willing to die for her or his benefit.) Now act according to the solution you have chosen. As soon as you do, you will more than likely find yourself confronted by a new conflict. And so the process begins again. That is what it means to live a faithful life of creative power and to assume social responsibility as a follower of Jesus Christ.

However, while imagination is essential for the creative use of power, there is no substitute for hard-nosed thinking. Too often the church has, with proper sensitivity and good will, sought to engage in the responsible use of power without having done the necessary homework. There is no place in the church for anti-intellectualism. Wisdom is essential for the Christian; and wisdom is the result of the difficult, time-consuming, sometimes frustrating use of the mind. While persons may become powerless while waiting to know everything necessary about a problem and its possible solu-. tions, persons may also compound present problems by running into a situation with a beautiful-sounding-unthought-out solution. I therefore, cannot over emphasize the importance of intellectual study before action. Finally, there is no substitute for knowledge and no responsible use of power without the use of the intellect.

One other quality possessed by the person of power needs to be mentioned. I call it the sense of urgency; the moral issue of time! To illustrate, let me tell you a story about some missionaries. These missionaries were concerned that the men with whom they were working treated their wives as property. They demanded that such a practice cease. The people agreed, but said it would take time. Concurrently the people were demanding that they receive equal pay for equal work at the mission station. The missionaries agreed, but said it would take time. Time is a moral issue, and a sense of urgency is essential to the life of faith, if love, power, and justice are to exist.

Now just as we need particular personal qualities to be a person of love, power, and justice, so do the communities, the voluntary associations, the churches to which we belong. We cannot be a person of power alone. We need a community of nurture and support. We need a group with which to act. Such a community is founded upon shared goals and understandings (faith). It is a community where there is open honest communication; conflict is handled creatively; care and respect for each person is realized in an atmosphere of trust; feedback and criticism are encouraged and accepted; accountability is maintained; openness to change and new ideas is supported; imagination, curiosity and creativity are valued; a healthy perspective on life is enhanced by a sense of humor; a feeling of fellowship abounds; and celebration is fundamental to the community's life.

To seek out and become involved in such a community of love, power, and justice is to possess those blessings for oneself. We each need a church of power if we are to be persons of power. And the world needs persons and churches of power also.

Guidelines

Before I proceed to outline a strategy for the responsible use of power through social action, let me acknowledge that there is no single theory of social change, no single strategy to be recommended above all others. The one which follows is simply one I have found valuable and effective. Others need to be explored and alternatives created. But first, a few notes relevant to the responsible use of power.

1. Avoid blaming the victims. It is not the poor's fault that they are poor. Correspondingly always see yourself as part of the problem. Never permit a "we the liberator" vs. "they the oppressed" to develop.

2. Permanent change is slow and gradual. While change will never be as fast as it morally ought to be, social change will tend to reverse itself unless it proceeds slowly enough to gain acceptance. For significant systemic change think five years, not one month. Be patient, but never lose a sense of urgency. They go together.

3. Don't fall in love with your solutions. Even the best laid plans of mice and persons often come to naught. Beware of negative consequences in your most creative ideas. Maintain a sense of humor. Don't take yourselves too seriously. Self-righteousness is a sin. Laugh at yourself.

4. Strive to see every problem through the eyes of the oppressed, repressed, suppressed person. Make sure they are involved in envisioning and acting for their good. Your responsibility is not to do things for others. That is patronizing and oppressive. You are to join with the outsider to create an alternative future.

5. Don't be as concerned to eliminate an evil as to create a good. Be aware of people's hurts but respond with visions.

6. It is terribly time-consuming always to be starting new groups to work on social problems. Use existing communities and organizations. Always involve as many people as possible.

7. Think innovation, a small acceptable addition to existing ways that will gradually cause significant change in the present system. When you eliminate things and force your ways upon others, it is self-defeating. Always have alternative solutions. And, of course, be willing to compromise.

8. Love your enemies. Never use violence. Have faith that you are not alone. Remember that both goals and means must be justified.

9. Periodically withdraw from your action. Seek a new perspective. Retreat to pray. Act and reflect. Reflect and act. Celebrate your little advances and even your reversals.

10. And most important, struggle daily with the Word of God as well as the problems of society. Live each day with your newspaper in one hand and the Bible in the other. Let the Scriptures judge and inspire your plans and actions. Take up your cross, but do all for the glory of God.

The responsible use of power for social change begins with a group of persons who are supported by a common faith and share a common concern. Don't try to solve all of the world's problems at once. Address one single manifestation of a social problem at a time. Make sure your group is willing to give single-minded attention, time, and energy to its solution.

Quite aware that social change necessitates coalitions of groups who share common goals, I am convinced that any initiating group needs also to share common faith and values. I believe the Christian faith supplies us with the necessary motivation for significant, purposeful social action. I also believe that the church is a community which can contribute much to meaningful social change. Of course the test of my convictions resides with congregations and their willingness to assume this responsibility and act upon their faith.

Any group desiring to effect change must agree on the problem to be addressed, the enemy to be conquered, the dream to be realized. Too often we address too many issues. As a result we effect none or so dissipate our energies that little is accomplished. While there is no need for a whole congregation to address the same issue, a variety of small groups can be formed, each with its own issue. Nevertheless, the congregation as a whole needs to encourage, support, and aid all the groups it spawns.

One of the greatest mistakes a congregation can make is to take a global issue like world poverty or racial justice and try to attack it in all its manifestations. The best way to address a global issue is to identify its manifestation in the place where you have the greatest power. I am convinced that if we effect change in one part of our social system we open up the possibility of change throughout the rest.

Last, if we are involved in too many enterprises no matter how noble, we will probably not have the time and energy to deal with any of them thoroughly; we will get tired before we have finished or lose out because our energies were too dissipated. We have to stop thinking that everyone needs to be personally involved in every cause. Pick the cause that concerns you most and about which you believe you will be able to exert the greatest power. Join with others. Give it your all. Encourage others to do the same.

Future Planning for Democratic Social Change

In the next few pages I will outline a strategy for the church to address social issues through the responsible use of power. I will use a single example to give the process some concreteness. For the sake of this illustration, pretend that you are a member of a small church in a university community. A number of your members are on the faculty and administration of the university. They and others, including a number of students who belong to the church, are concerned about social issues related to higher education.

A. DEVELOP A FUTURE SCENARIO

1. Assuming a common issue or concern to be addressed, each person should write a personal vision (I recommend a newspaper account). It should be brief, precise, and concrete. It should focus on a single issue or concern in some effectable manifestation. Example: Education is the issue, our state system of higher education an effectable manifestation.

   These scenarios should be truly visionary. Not the future anyone thinks *can be* or the future anyone thinks is *apt to be,* but the future for which someone *hopes.* Encourage persons to free themselves from the present—its restrictions, demands, crises, problems, frustrations. Have persons dream five years from the present and describe their vision. What is going on; where; how; with whom; for what purposes? For example, one part of a future scenario might read: "Beginning today every high school graduate in our state has the opportunity to continue his or her education, without cost, regardless of race, sex, national origin, or how well he or she did academically or socially during his or her high school years."

2. Once all persons in the group have completed their personal scenarios, these should be duplicated and distributed to the group. Each person should be directed to read all of them carefully, underlining or noting those aspects of each one that is especially appealing.

3. After this task is completed, some one or two persons

from the group should be given the responsibility to review and unite the various visionary statements into a composite group scenario.

4. The group then needs to review, discuss, evaluate, rework, and finally approve and own a future group scenario. Copies should be made and distributed to each member. Celebration is now appropriate.

B. ESTABLISH GOALS

1. Still living in your hoped-for future, the group should organize its group scenarios into a series of summary statements. Each statement should clearly describe one aspect of the group vision. Write these as goals—ends desired. For example, previously we used the illustration "Beginning today every high school graduate in our state has the opportunity to continue his or her education, without cost, regardless of race, sex, national origin, or how well he or she did academically or socially during his or her high school years." Consistent with that vision a goal statement might read ALL STATE UNIVERSITIES HAVE AN OPEN ADMISSION POLICY. Write as many goals as necessary.

2. Now discuss these goals. Encourage persons to advocate particular goals as being most important to the overall vision of the group. Next have each person rank order each goal using the criteria of significance for the group's visionary future and their own personal preference. Tabulate these rank orderings and establish which five goals are considered most important to the group.

3. Have each person write a sentence describing what it will look like and what will be occurring when each of these five goals is reached. For example, if one of your goals was "All state universities have an open admissions policy" one person might write, ALL HIGH

SCHOOL GRADUATES WHO HOLD A HIGH SCHOOL DIPLOMA
ARE ENCOURAGED TO MATRICULATE INTO ANY STATE UNI-
VERSITY WITHOUT HAVING TO MEET ANY OTHER ENTRANCE
REQUIREMENTS.

4. Share these descriptive paragraphs. Did everyone understand each goal well enough to describe it? Did
everyone agree what the goal would look like when it
is realized? And did these descriptions correspond to
the group's future vision? If so, proceed. If not, discuss
the goals and rework them until everyone is clear.

5. There is always a price to be paid by the achievement
of any goal. Sometimes these consequences are negative
and sometimes positive. If we do not consider consequences, our goals may prove to be nightmares. Positive consequences can help us decide priorities. An
awareness of negative consequences can help us plan
more wisely and thereby avoid disaster.

The group should, therefore, take each of the five
priority goals and list as many positive and negative
consequences for each as possible. For example, using
the goal in our earlier illustration, positive consequences might be listed as follows: "A higher per-
centage of lower-class Black and Chicano youth get a
chance to attend college; 'late bloomers' have an opportunity to acquire college degrees; and a better
educated public ensues." Negative consequences might
be listed as: "a poorer class of students complicate college teaching; professors might leave public institutions
for more selective private ones; and university costs
might spiral."

6. Next evaluate the consequences. Using these evalua-
tions as criteria, have each person vote on their two
most preferred goals. Establish the one highest priority
goal. Own that goal as the group's single most im-

portant desire for the future. Copies should be duplicated and distributed. Celebration is once again appropriate.

C. LIST FUTURE EVENTS

1. With the group's future goal in mind, have the group return in their thinking to one year from the present. List all the events that can be imagined, which if they occurred in one year would contribute toward the achievement of that goal. For example, using the same goal as in our previous illustration, a list of future events might include: "A remedial curriculum is developed; increased budgets for state universities are voted; faculty interested in teaching high risk students are hired; high school and university counselors are trained to interpret open admissions and aid high risk students; and a trial experiment in open admissions is voted." Follow the rules of brainstorming. Record all ideas no matter how wild they may appear. Do not permit anyone to judge another's idea.

2. Once you have a list of possible future events, evaluate each according to the following criteria:
   a. it will significantly contribute to the goal.
   b. it is an event we can conceive as occurring in one year from the present.
   c. it is an event that has value to us and a significant proportion of those necessary for its realization.
   d. it is an event we believe we can help realize.
   (Eliminate all those that do not meet these four criteria.)

3. Next have each person rank order the remaining future events using the criteria of significance to the group's goal and their personal preference. Based upon this rank ordering, establish those two future events of greatest importance to your group. Own them. Copy and distribute. Celebrate.

D. WRITE ACTION OBJECTIVES

1. Take your group's two future events and rewrite them as a clearly stated objective. For example, if one future event is related to the development of a remedial curriculum, an action objective might read: "By 1977 a comprehensive curriculum to meet diverse individual learning needs of freshpersons is developed."

2. Review your objectives. Are they clear and precise? Does everyone understand them in the same way? Does everyone like the picture of education they represent? Do you believe that they will help reach your group's long-range goal? Does everyone in your group desire them enough to commit their time and energy to their realization? If so, the group is ready to proceed. If not, the group may have to rewrite or establish alternative events and objectives.

E. ANALYZE THE SITUATION

1. Your group is now ready to move back into the present. Take each of your group's objectives and brainstorm for forces which will encourage the attainment of objectives and forces which will discourage each from being reached. Forces include items such as: individual and group interest, community values, past history, costs, time, laws, and policies. For example, using the illustration of a remedial curriculum, encouraging forces might be listed as: "Federal funds available for such projects; a core of faculty is concerned and interested; and good experience in other state universities." Discouraging forces might be listed as: "the provost of the university opposes the idea; and faculty is already overworked."

2. Establish which of the negative forces should be modified and which of the positive forces should be encouraged if the objective is to be realized.

F. DEVELOP ALTERNATIVE STRATEGIES

  1. In the light of insights gained in the analysis of the situation, alternative strategies or general overall courses of action need to be explored. For example:

     a. demand that the president and trustees replace the provost; grant power to a student-faculty committee to establish a new curriculum; provide funds; release faculty from other responsibilities and give students academic credit for their help

     b. recommend to the president that the college hire an outside consulting firm to create a new curriculum for high risk students

     c. call a group of concerned faculty, students and administrators together to develop a proposal for federal funding of a curriculum project; send a small group to investigate programs at other universities and begin a small pilot project for high risk students

  2. Evaluate each strategy by the following criteria or other criteria which the group deems important:

     a. dollar cost

     b. time

     c. necessary human resources

     d. possible negative side effects

     e. chance of success

     f. individuals or groups who will oppose or support the strategy

  3. Decide on one strategy or a combination of two.

G. DECIDE ACTION STEPS

  1. Your group is now ready to prepare detailed precise steps in an action plan. These steps can be as elaborate or as simple as your group feels is suitable to its style and needs. But elaborate or simple, the steps need to be specific about people, times, and costs. Each step should include WHO, will do WHAT, by WHEN, for what PURPOSE.

  2. Act!

H. Evaluate . . . Plan Again . . . Continue to Act

Build in a time schedule, criteria and a means for evaluating your group's work. Review your accomplishments and consider changing needs. Reflect on your vision. Change when necessary. Continue to reaffirm or rework your group's vision. Do the same with future events. Add new ones as existing ones are achieved. Keep planning. Keep acting. Keep reflecting!

Maintain faith and hope and love. Celebrate God's actions in history! Keep dreaming of God's kingdom-coming. Keep doing the Word. Use the power God has granted you to responsibly address social issues and produce social change consistent with your understanding of God's kingdom. And may the blessing of God the Creator, Redeemer, and Sustainer be with you now and forever. Amen.

Chapter Five

Education
Learning to Act As Christians

The greatest challenge of my ministry has been to enable the church to become a witnessing community of faith in the world. I have prayed and I have worked to motivate the church, as an expression of its faith, to engage in democratic social change. For years I have tried to create educational designs which would equip groups in churches for responsible Christian social action.

While preparing to write this book I reflected on those attempts. Some interesting observations surfaced. My first attempts, I discovered, were primarily focused on thinking, information, and knowledge. Understanding social issues and understanding God's Word were central to the learning process in those days. I still believe that thinking and understanding are important, but I have learned that they, alone, are not adequate for my goals.

Having sensed the inadequacy of thinking, I next turned to feelings. Living God's Word in small groups seemed to be the answer. Like others, I assumed that if we centered learning on people's attitudes and feelings, they would act differently. I am still convinced that feelings play a crucial role in Christian faith and life, but I have learned that even when feelings are combined with thinking, persons are not motivated or equipped for social action.

In retrospect, I find the next stage in my life to be re-actionary. Having all but discarded thinking and feeling, I moved to designing education exclusively for action. Learning techniques were borrowed from the political-social activists and radical secularists. As you might expect, these attempts also failed, but for different reasons. Focusing on society to the exclusion of tradition and persons was no more helpful in reaching my goals than my previous efforts.

I know now that Christian education has to unite concerns for tradition, persons, and society, with concerns about how people think, feel, and act. God's Word must be known, understood, lived, and acted upon. At the heart of all of our educational efforts must be the Scriptures. At the same time we cannot afford to ignore the spiritual needs of persons. Prayer and the religious affections need to be nurtured and people's emotions and feelings ministered to by small groups that live their faith in intimate, caring communities. But neither can we forget the importance of preparing persons for their Christian vocation in society. Equipping persons and groups for social action cannot be avoided if education is to be Christian.

As I reflected on ways to unite these educational concerns with the foundations laid in the previous chapters, I concluded that our educational goal is best expressed as enabling groups of persons to *do* God's Word. To accomplish this end, I believe we will need to focus our educational efforts on the will—that is, to facilitate groups of persons to act with passion, after thoughtful reflection, in society, on behalf of God's kingdom-coming. Doing the Word implies understanding and living the Word. The will unites thinking, feeling, and acting. The educational model which follows is built upon these affirmations. But just as there is no single model for social change, there is no single model for responsible Christian social action education. Mine is only one of many that need to be developed; my hope is that it will help and stimulate you to create others.

The model which follows is a learning model. Its goal is not to achieve significant social change (though that may hopefully occur) but to help groups learn how, as Christians, they can assume social responsibility and act for change in society, consistent with the gospel. I have tried to take seriously the learning needs surfaced in my chapters on Shipbuilding, Visions, Hope, and Power. A worshiping, learning, caring, witnessing community of faith, memory, hope, and power is affirmed as basic to the learning process and is made the focus of this model.

As you will see, the model is expressed as steps in a process. These steps are not lessons to be taught in a classroom to existing church school classes. They are parts of an educational process for a self-selected group of no more than twelve older youth and/or adults. Each step and order is important. However, depending on the nature of your group, particular steps may have to be expanded into two or more learning occasions. As I present them, each step requires a one- or two-hour block of time. Regular attendance is essential.

There are ten steps. Step eight is expected to need two or more sessions. The model is therefore based upon weekly meetings for three months. However, steps one through eight can be meaningfully accomplished on a three-day retreat or two weekend retreats with meetings thereafter for steps nine and ten.

I have suggested environments, resources, and learning experiences consistent with the aim of each step, but you may find that they are not usable with your people. No problem. Create your own. The educational designs I describe in this model have worked well for me; they may not be best for you. Do not follow them rigidly.

Each step is an educational design which includes aims, theological and educational assumptions, needed resources, and procedures. Together these ten educational designs comprise a model of church education for social responsibility.

Step One—Announcement

Aim

To secure persons to participate in a series of learning experiences whose goal is to equip and motivate them to engage in social change through responsible Christian social action.

Assumptions

1. While this educational program is appropriate for all youth and adults, it is important that persons make a personal decision to participate.
2. Both commitment and preparation are essential for significant learning.

Resources

1. A poster (s) to be placed on the church bulletin board (s) or a notice to be run in the church bulletin: WANTED: Persons who are troubled by their inability to put their faith into action. Persons who are committed to social justice, liberation, peace, unity, and well-being of all humanity. Persons who care enough about social injustice, oppression, racism, poverty, hunger, sexism, discord and war to dedicate at least one evening each week for three months to equip themselves for responsible Christian social action.
   Sign up: (where, when, how, with whom).
2. Directions for daily preparation prior to the first meeting of the group.
   Each day take time to withdraw by yourself. Read the daily newspaper from cover to cover.
   Read: Exodus 15:1–21

1 Samuel 2:1–10
Judith 9:11–12
Luke 1:46–53

(You may want to duplicate these passages. If so, *The New English Bible* is recommended.)

Pray the following prayer:

God, parent of my Lord Jesus Christ and my parent. My days are haunted and my nights tormented because your kingdom has not come in all its glory. I confess that I live in a world that denies justice, liberation, unity, well-being, community and peace to your children; and I confess that I daily contribute to the denial of your will. Make me ready for your kingdom's coming. Grant me visions of your future and renew my memories of your past actions. Do not let me rest until I have been trained in your kingdom-building. In the name of Jesus Christ your crucified and risen offspring, I pray. Amen.

3. Secure a copy of *Tomorrow's Church* for each member of the group. IMPORTANT: These are not to be distributed or read before the beginning of step nine.

Procedure

1. Publicize the program.
2. Sign-up participants.
3. Give participants the directions for home preparation.
4. Form one or more groups as needed. Groups should not have more than twelve or fewer than six persons.
5. Read through the entire educational model. Note needed preparations. Commit yourself to leading the group.
6. Determine and announce the date, time and place of the first and subsequent meetings. Explain that total commitment is essential and that attendance at all meetings is expected. Suggest that no one attend the first meeting who does not intend to be faithful.

(It is best to have at least two weeks between the date

that directions for preparation are passed out and the first meeting.)

Step Two—Community Building

Aim

To build community and secure commitment.

Assumptions

1. Because we cannot be Christian alone, there is no Christian social action without community.
2. Community in the church cannot be assumed.
3. Christian community is founded upon a shared faith-story, a shared fellowship with a living God, and a shared commitment to common goals for action.
4. Worship is important for the formation of Christian community.

Resources

1. A comfortable room with a rug where people can sit on the floor.
2. Four paintings of the crucifixion, with lights that can be directed on them, but easily turned on and off. One painting should be placed on each of the four walls in which you will be meeting, at a level easily seen when seated.
3. A small, low table with a cross and burning candles.
4. One large, plain sweet roll and a mug of hot coffee with cream and sugar for each person, prepared and ready to pass out just before the beginning of the meeting.
5. A Bible (*The New English Bible* is recommended).
6. A record player or tape recorder with a recording of the "Credo" from Bach's *B Minor Mass*.

7. Hymn books or mimeographed hymns.
8. A 10″ candle for each person.

Procedure

1. When people arrive the room should be darkened with the exception of the lit candles on the table. Every person on arrival is given another candle. Instruct them to light their candle from the table candles and sit in a circle around the table for a moment of meditation and prayer.

2. Lead the following Liturgy (It is based upon a Moravian Love Feast).

   Hymn: "O Master Let Me Walk with Thee"
   Scripture: James 2:14–26
   Hymn: "He Who Would Valiant Be" (Use she on alternate verses.)
   Scripture: Exodus 15:1–21
       1 Samuel 2:1–10
       Luke 1:46–53
   Prayer: (in unison) Use the prayer from step one.
   Hymn: "When I Survey the Wondrous Cross" (Light the crucifix paintings.)
   Meditation—Love Feast (Pass out the coffee and rolls. Play the "Credo.") Maintain silence. At the close, put out the lights on the crucifix paintings.
   Sharing: In pairs have each person share the story of how they became the person of faith they are now. Have each person introduce their neighbor in the light of their faith biography.
   Hymn: "God of Grace and God of Glory"
   Scripture: Acts 2:42–47
   Discussion:

   a. Have each person, beginning with yourself, retell in his or her own words the Acts account, as if it were your own story.

b. After everyone has shared in retelling the Acts story, give each person an opportunity to share the "marvels and signs" revealed to them during their lifetimes by Christ's faithful people.

Hymn: "Once to Every Person and Nation"
Commission:

a. Have each person, one at a time, express what they intend to give of themselves to the community and its endeavors in terms of commitment, time, and talents.

b. After all have finished, have them kneel and let everyone place their hands on the kneeling one's head. As they do you say: "(Name), we commission you in the name of Jesus Christ to (repeat what they said) and we promise to support you and to hold you accountable. Amen."

Benediction: (Following the benediction have everybody extinguish their candles.)

Kiss of Peace: (Following the kiss of peace instruct everyone to leave in silence and to remain silent until they reach home.)

Step Three—Owning God's Vision

Aim

To understand and own God's intentions of liberation, justice, community, unity, well-being, and peace for all humanity.

Assumptions

1. Christian education for social action begins with the biblical vision of God's *shalom* kingdom.

2. Understanding is not complete until experience is reflected upon and verbalized or until verbal statements

are reflected upon and expressed nonverbally. The arts, therefore, can play an important role in biblical study and interpretation.

Resources

1. Open space for dramatic activity.
2. Refreshments.
3. A copy of the following biblical passages for each person:

I will give you rain at the proper time; the land shall yield its produce and the trees of the country-side their fruit. Threshing shall last till vintage and vintage till sowing; you shall eat your fill and live secure in your land (Lev. 26:4–6).

> They shall beat their swords into mattocks
>   and their spears into pruning-knives;
> nation shall not lift up sword against nation
>   nor ever again be trained for war.
>
> (Isa. 2:4)

They shall know that I am the Lord when I break the bars of their yokes and rescue them from those who have enslaved them. . . . I will give prosperity to their plantations; they shall never again be victims of famine in the land nor any longer bear the taunts of the nations (Ezek. 34:27, 29).

The arrogant of heart and mind he has put to rout,
he has brought down monarchs from their thrones,
    but the humble have been lifted high.
The hungry he has satisfied with good things,
    the rich sent empty away.

(Luke 1:51–53)

Then I saw a new heaven and a new earth, for the first heaven and the first earth had vanished, and there was no longer any sea. I saw the holy city, new Jerusalem, coming down out of heaven from God, made ready like a bride adorned for her husband. I heard a loud voice proclaiming from the throne: "Now at last God has his dwelling among persons! He will dwell among them and they shall be his people, and God himself will be with them. He will wipe every tear from their eyes; there shall be an end to death, and to mourning and crying and pain; for the old order has passed away! (Rev. 21:1–4).

Procedure

1. Distribute copies of the biblical passages.
2. Instruct each person to reflect on the passages and write a paragraph describing concretely what it will look like when these passages are fulfilled in the lives of all people—especially Black, Spanish-speaking, Oriental and first Americans in this country and third-world people throughout the world.
3. Take one biblical passage at a time and have each person share his or her paragraphs with the group.
4. Discuss each biblical passage in the light of these descriptions. Strive to find a single word to characterize each passage.
5. Together create a nonverbal dramatic expression combining all the biblical passages into a single vision for the world. Be original. Demonstrate that you understand the meaning and implications of the combined biblical passages.
6. Have a celebration.

   Song: "Kum Ba Yah"

   Scripture: Read the passages used this evening.

   Response: Reenact your drama.

   Prayer: God of all people and all history. We celebrate with all the heavenly host your vision for humanity. Tonight we commit our lives and actions to your will, and pray that you will hold us up in our striving after your vision. *Marana tha.* Come, O Lord. Amen.

7. Refreshments.

Step Four—Visions and Reality

Aims

1. To express personal visions for life consistent with God's vision.
2. To express personal understandings of reality as it compares with those visions.

Assumptions

1. It is important to concretize and personalize significant aspects of God's vision as it relates to people's daily lives.
2. It is important to acknowledge the way life is and contrast our visions with reality.
3. The arts are important for learning, and especially for expressing and sharing thoughts and feelings.

Resources

1. Materials for painting, sculpture, and collages.
2. Refreshments.

Procedure

1. Each person is to create a piece of art (it can be a painting, sculpture, a montage, or collage made from materials or magazines; it can be abstract, or pictorial) consistent with God's vision for all humanity, concrete in terms of where they live, and desired by them. For example, by reflecting on God's vision I might choose justice as being most important to me. Then reflecting on the situation where I live, I might envision the need for prison reform. Therefore, I might paint a

picture symbolizing the release of hundreds of prisoners, mostly Black, from their death row cells.

Convince them that it is not important to be a
"good" artist. Encourage people.

2. Have each person also create a second piece of art
symbolizing the reality of their situation. For example,
I might paint a picture symbolizing hundreds of lonely,
isolated persons in death row cells for years on end.

3. Create an art gallery. If possible put it somewhere in
your church, where it can remain for a few weeks. Keep
visions and reality by the same artist together. Title
them if you wish. Title the total exhibit: "Visions
and Realities."

4. Serve refreshments and conduct gallery talks. Together,
go from one set of creations to another. Discuss them
with the artist. Enjoy yourselves.

Step Five—Recalling the Story

Aim

To call to memory the actions of God in history on behalf of the *shalom* kingdom.

Assumptions

1. Ritual is one of the best ways to recover our memory
and relive our history.

2. Faced by visions and reality it is important to recall
God's continuing action in history on behalf of the
biblical vision for all humanity.

Resources

1. A copy of Arthur L. Waskow, *The Freedom Seder,*
Holt, Rinehart, and Winston, 1970, $3.95, or *The
Union Prayerbook for Jewish Worship.*

2. If you use the alternative source for your Seder, I rec-

ommend that you use the following story from Waskow's *The Freedom Seder.* It comes after the question
"Why is this night different from all other nights?

Moses lived in a period of dictatorship. Our people
were slaves. The bosses made them work under a speed-
up system, and committed horrible atrocities, such as
trying to kill all the boy-babies born to our people.

Moses himself was saved from such a death only be-
cause his mother hid him in a reed basket in the Nile
River. There he was found by the daughter of the
Pharaoh, which is what they called their dictator in
Egypt. The princess took Moses to the royal palace and
had him brought up as her son.

When Moses was a young man he became curious
about the Hebrew slaves, and one day went to the
brickyards where some of them were working. The first
thing he saw was an Egyptian boss hitting a Hebrew
laborer. Moses was a powerful young man. He lost his
temper. He hit the boss—and killed him! He buried the
body hastily in the sand and went back to the palace.

But a fire was kindled in Moses' heart, a fire of concern about his people and their suffering. The next day
he went back to the hot brickyards. Then he learned
two things that those who try to help their fellows
often discover.

He found first that slaves often spend as much time
and energy fighting each other as they do their common
oppressors, and second, that slaves do not always wel-
come their deliverers. They get accustomed to being
slaves. Even after they have been freed, if freedom
brings hardship, they may want to return "to the flesh
pots of Egypt."

This time Moses found two Hebrews fighting each
other. When he rebuked them, they turned on him and
said, "Who made you our boss? Do you mean to kill us
as you did that Egyptian yesterday?"

Moses feared that in order to turn suspicion away
from themselves they would tell the Egyptians that he
killed the boss. He concluded that it might not be

healthy to stay around those parts, so he ran away. He settled down to a nice comfortable life, raising a family and feeding the flocks of his father-in-law.

Only after a while God came into the picture. What was the sign that God had come? It was a bush that burned and burned and did not stop burning. Moses had had a fire kindled in his heart once, but it went out or at least died down. God is the Being whose heart does not stop burning, in whom the flame does not die down.

What was God all burned up about? The voice that came out of the bush said, "I have seen the affliction of my people that are in Egypt and have heard their cry by reason of their oppressors." It was the physical, economic, and spiritual suffering, the injustice, the degradation to which actual people were subjected here on earth that caused God's concern.

And the proof that God had entered into Moses, and that Moses had really been "converted," was that he had to go back and identify himself with his enslaved people—organize them into Brickmakers' Union Number One—and lead them out of hunger and slavery into freedom and into "a good land and a large land flowing with milk and honey."

At the head of the Ten Commandments stand these great words: "I am the Lord thy God which has brought thee out of the land of Egypt, out of the slave-house. Thou shalt have no other Gods before me"—before this God who is in the hearts of his prophets as the Eternal Flame that will not let them rest where there is injustice and inequality until these have been done away with and people set about building God's House instead of the slave-house.

To be religious, our foreparents discovered, is to get out of Egypt into Canaan; to refuse to be slaves or contented draft-horses; to build brotherhood and sisterhood in freedom—because that is what people, the children of God, were created to do! And religious leaders are those who identify themselves with the oppressed, so that men and women may carry out this, their true mission in the world. (Quoted from the prophet Abraham Johannes Muste in Waskow, *The Freedom Seder,* pp. 4–8. Used by permission.)

3. Seder items:
   a. A table that everyone can sit around.
   b. A plate with three sheets of Matzah covered by a napkin.
   c. Two unlit candles and matches.
   d. A bowl of vinegar.
   e. A bowl of plain water for washing.
   f. A cup of wine for each person.
   g. Flowers for the table.
   h. A cup and a bottle of wine, and an empty cup to be filled for Elijah.
   i. A plate with an egg, a burnt chicken bone, sliced raw horseradish, a quantity of ground horseradish, sprigs of parsley, and a quantity of charoset (a mixture of chopped nuts and apples with wine).
   j. Food for a meal.

Procedure

1. Secure, long in advance, a copy of Waskow's *The Freedom Seder* (or an alternative). Read it carefully; adapt it where necessary for your use. Prepare to lead the service.
2. Hold a Seder.

Step Six—Naming the Principalities and Powers

Aim

1. To establish a group vision consistent with God's vision for the world.
2. To identify the single most important political, social,

or economic force preventing your group's vision from being actualized.

Assumptions

1. It is important for a group to identify and own a common, concrete expression of God's vision before engaging in social action.
2. It is necessary that groups engaged in the responsible use of power identify those political, social and economic forces which prevent the realization of their visions.

Resources

1. The art exhibit "Visions and Realities."
2. Newsprint, masking tape, and magic markers.
3. Song books and a guitar player or hymn books and a piano player.
4. Refreshments.

Procedure

1. If necessary, set up your "Visions and Realities" exhibit again. Have refreshments when people arrive and encourage everyone to familiarize themselves with the themes of the paintings and sculptures.
2. Conduct an old-fashioned hymn sing or a contemporary folk concert.
3. Corporately make a list of all the visions contained in your works of art. Discuss them.
4. Have each person rank-order the visions according to personal preference. Tabulate the rank orderings to establish the one vision most important to the group. Seek ownership for that vision. Commit yourselves to its realization.
5. Make two lists on newsprint. On the first, list all the political, social, and economic forces that are encouraging the fulfillment of your vision. On the second, list all those which are discouraging the fulfillment of your vision.

Explain that political, social, and economic forces are for example: municipal by-laws, church structures, slum landlords, school boards, cultural differences, family expectations, denominationalism, state laws, housing patterns, historic prejudice, political machines, corporate organizations, single industry towns, high level of unemployment, and income differentials.

6. Discuss the list of negative forces. Clarify and combine where possible. Establish which one discouraging force most needs to be addressed if your vision is to be achieved.

7. Sing more hymns or folk songs.

8. Read:

I am God, and there is no one like me;
I reveal the end from the beginning,
from ancient times I reveal what is to be;
I say, "My purpose shall take effect,
I will accomplish all that I please" (Isa. 46:9–10).

He has made known to us his hidden purpose—such was his will and pleasure determined beforehand in Christ—to be put into effect when the time was ripe: namely, that the universe, all in heaven and on earth, might be brought into a unity in Christ (Eph. 1:9–10).

On that cross he discarded the cosmic powers and authorities like a garment; he made a public spectacle of them and led them as captives in his triumphal procession (Col. 2:15).

For I am convinced that there is nothing in death or life, in the realm of spirits or superhuman powers, in the world as it is or the world as it shall be, in the forces of the universe, in heights and depths—nothing in all creation that can separate us from the love of God in Christ Jesus our Lord (Rom. 8:38–39).

9. Have one or more persons read off the list of forces encouraging your vision. Give a shout of joy!

And offer a prayer of thanksgiving.
10. Close the evening with joyful singing.

Step Seven—Freeing Our Wills

Aims

1. To identify those personal psychological forces which prevent us from acting upon our social visions.
2. To liberate persons from their personal hang-ups so they may act freely on behalf of the group's social vision.

Assumptions

1. It is necessary to free persons from their personal, psychological hang-ups if they are to engage in social action.
2. Faith in Christ Jesus makes possible liberation from our psychological captivities.

Resources

1. Bible.
2. Paper and pencils for each person.
3. Party decorations.
4. A cup of salt.
5. A record player and joyful celebration music.
6. Refreshments.

Procedure

1. Ask each person to make a list of the psychological hang-ups which are likely to prevent them from acting boldly on behalf of your group's vision. Give examples such as fear of losing friends, lack of courage to take a stand, love of money and security, prejudices, the tendency to procrastinate and fear of failure.

2. Read Mark 10:46–52.

   They came to Jericho; and as he was leaving the town, with his disciples and a large crowd, Bartimaeus son of Timaeus, a blind beggar, was seated at the roadside. Hearing that it was Jesus of Nazareth, he began to shout, "Son of David, Jesus, have pity on me!" Many of the people told him to hold his tongue; but he shouted all the more, "Son of David, have pity on me." Jesus stopped and said, "Call him"; so they called the blind man and said, "Take heart; stand up; he is calling you." At that he threw off his cloak, sprang up, and came to Jesus. Jesus said to him, "What do you want me to do for you?" "Master," the blind man answered, "I want my sight back." Jesus said to him, "Go; your faith has cured you." And at once he recovered his sight and followed him on the road (Mark 10:46–52).

3. Ask each person to identify with Bartimaeus the blind beggar. Suggest that they substitute all of their psychological hang-ups for the blindness of Bartimaeus. Have each person write a poem telling Jesus specifically what they want him to do for them, namely, take away their hang-ups so that they will be free to do God's will. Direct them to end the poem with the refrain "I'm free! I'm free!"

4. Share your poems.

5. Once again read Mark 10:46–52.

6. Words of healing (leader):

   "My brothers and sisters, God has come to us in Jesus Christ to take away our blindness and grant us newness of life. Therefore I announce in the name of Christ that our confessed sins are forgiven according to the gospel. By faith we are free from all psychological hang-ups. Our faith has made us whole. God has given us the power to pick up our crosses and follow Christ our Lord. We are liberated to do God's will. Hallelujah! Amen."

7. Pass the cup of salt. Have each person put a pinch of salt on their tongue and as they do their neighbor should say:

"Go forth as a new person in Christ, to do God's will, remembering that you are called to be the salt of the earth. Amen."

8. Turn on the music. Decorate the room for a party. Eat, drink, and be merry. Celebrate your new freedom and commitment.

Step Eight—Planning to Act

Aim

To develop an action plan for addressing the negative political, social, or economic force which prevents your group's vision of God's kingdom from being realized.

Assumptions

1. This step will take two or more sessions.
2. Responsible Christian social action is a result of careful planning.
3. Future's planning (see chapter four) suggests a meaningful, effective process for engaging in social change.

Resources

Mimeograph copies of the "Future's Planning Guide" found on pages 97f. in *Tomorrow's Church*. Add extra plain worksheets.

Procedure

Follow the step-by-step procedures outlined in the "Future's Planning Guide." Begin with the creation of a vision. Use as the object of your hoped-for vision of the future, your discouraging political, social, or economic force identified in step six.

Step Nine—Acting in the World

Aim

1. To engage in social action according to plans made in step eight.
2. To celebrate your acts of social responsibility.

Assumptions

1. Group social action is essential to the responsible use of power.
2. A small change in the social system consistent with God's vision for the world and God's will makes a difference to God's kingdom-coming.
3. Liturgy is important to motivate and sustain social action.

Resources

1. Your Future's Planning workbook.
2. Bible.
3. Two boxes at least four-by-four feet.
4. A black cloth.
5. A bottle of wine, a chalice, and a loaf of uncut, home-made bread.
6. Straight pins.
7. Two sheets of nine-by-twelve-inch colored paper for each person.
8. Crayons for each person.
9. An ordained minister for the celebration. Prepare this person by explaining the celebration and by asking him to conduct the Eucharist in the celebration.

Procedure

1. Begin to act according to your action plan.
2. After about two weeks of action plan to gather for a celebration.

3. Arrange the room so that when people arrive, the two boxes are in the middle of the room, one on top of the other. Under the top box, out of sight, place the wine, bread and chalice.

4. As people arrive, instruct them to put one word and a symbol or drawing of the vision they are acting for on one piece of paper. Have them do the same thing with the reality they are trying to effect in the vision.

5. Have everyone pin their visions on the outside of the boxes.

6. Remind them that visions are important, but that realities must be faced. Put the black cloth over the boxes and have everyone pin their reality papers on the cloth.

7. Ask everyone to hold hands and make a circle.
   Read the following passages from the Bible:
   Leviticus 26:4–6
   Isaiah 2:4
   Ezekiel 34:27–29
   Luke 1:52–53
   Revelation 21:1–4
   Zechariah 9:9

8. As you finish with the last reading begin to sing the Doxology. As everyone joins in, throw off the black cloth, take the top box and place it next to the bottom box, making an altar out of them and revealing the wine, bread, and chalice.

9. Remind the group that the Eucharist is the victory party of the people of God who even in evil days can sing and dance knowing that they act with God and that the principalities and powers are finally defeated. Share the kiss of peace.

10. Have the minister consecrate the elements and as they are passed among the people lead everyone in continual, joyous singing and dancing.

11. Share in community intercessions. Commission each other to continue actions in the world and pronounce

the benediction. Let the party continue until all the bread and wine are consumed.

Step Ten—Reflections and Decisions

Aim

1. To reflect on your actions.
2. To surface learnings through discussions on the church, visions, hope, and power.
3. To make a decision on future actions.

Assumptions

1. Learning is a result of action and reflection.
2. The most meaningful context in which to discuss the contents of *Tomorrow's Church* is in the midst of social involvement.

Resources

1. A copy of *Tomorrow's Church* for each person.
2. Bible.
3. Hymn books.
4. Refreshments.

Procedure

1. Pass out *Tomorrow's Church* and suggest that everyone read the first four chapters.
2. Meet regularly during the time in which you are engaged in action to discuss the contents of this book in the light of your experience.
3. Each time you meet, read from the Scriptures, pray, and sing hymns together. Share each other's burdens and care for each other's needs. Commit yourself to act. And return to the world with hope.
4. After you have finished the book, reflect on your

learnings and growth in faith. Celebrate together. Decide on what you intend to do next. Consider ways to interest others in your church in similar learning experiences. Act—reflect—and act again.

And so the learning process continues. In a sense it must never end. As persons become more sure of their faith, as they gain a deeper sense of hope and begin to sense the power God has given them, their commitment to act should increase and their actions become more significant and effective. But learning to act for democratic social change continues.

Tomorrow's Church was written as a resource for Christian social action, but learning does not begin or end with a book. I only hope that it has provided you with a guide for creating new forms of Christian education in your church. The final test will be the degree to which your church is more faithfully and significantly involved in the world, for to that end it was written.

Postscript

No more time to contemplate and pray, to reflect and write. My holiday has ended. These have been holy days; I am rested and refreshed, stimulated and anxious to get back to the challenges and responsibilities of Duke University and Durham, North Carolina. I would be lying, however, to say that I will not miss this place. It is difficult to leave these mountains and lakes where unity and community, well-being and peace seem so natural and to return to the sidewalks, the hovels and the highrises of "civilization" where discord and poverty, oppression and injustice seem equally natural. But I do so with a new vision, a renewed hope, and a promise to myself and God to live more responsibly. I am quite aware that I cannot do that alone and so I also return with an increased commitment to both my family and to Christ and his church. You see, the only way I can justify having had these harmonious, happy days of good food and drink, companionship and friends, freedom and peace is by using the strength, wisdom, health, and wholeness I've gained in the struggle to bring these blessings to those who have been denied them.

This book is my first contribution to that end.

A few moments ago I reread this manuscript, begun just two weeks ago. It is uneven, sometimes it repeats itself and often it lacks the precision and depth that only more time can provide. I wrote this book because I had to write it and now I must move on to act. Enough words have been used already. I pray they will make a difference to the oppressed, hurt, marginal people of our world. If not, then this has been an academic escape into irrelevance, for while it was not written for them, it was written on their behalf.

As a professor, I have done what professors do; I have professed what I believe at this moment in order to stimulate you to think and act for yourselves. That is why I encouraged you to write your book as you read and react to mine. My efforts will be justified if you have a clearer understanding and commitment to the biblical vision of God's kingdom; if you have a renewed hope in Christ that the struggle for the unity, peace, well-being, community, justice, and liberation of all humanity is worthwhile; if you have a deeper commitment to do the Word and will of God through responsible social action; and if you have a helpful design for Christian education to aid your faith community to be more responsible advocates of and actors in God's kingdom-coming. If that dream in some way has been met then this little book on shipbuilding will have made a contribution to the life of the shipfaring people of God.

Marana tha—Come, O Lord!

The grace of the Lord Jesus Christ, and the love of God, and the fellowship of the Holy Spirit, be with us all, my sisters and brothers. Amen.